D1483950

THE MUSIC TREE

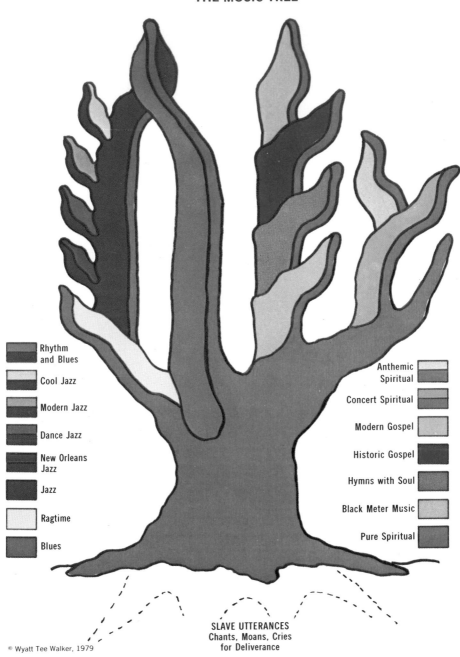

Rhythm and Blues

Cool Jazz

Modern Jazz

Dance Jazz

New Orleans Jazz

Jazz

Ragtime

Blues

Anthemic Spiritual

Concert Spiritual

Modern Gospel

Historic Gospel

Hymns with Soul

Black Meter Music

Pure Spiritual

SLAVE UTTERANCES
Chants, Moans, Cries
for Deliverance

© Wyatt Tee Walker, 1979

"Somebody's Calling My Name"

ATS
781.62
W 15

"Somebody's Calling My Name"

Black Sacred Music and Social Change

Wyatt Tee Walker

Judson Press® Valley Forge

17795

4932902

"SOMEBODY'S CALLING MY NAME"

Copyright © 1979
Judson Press, Valley Forge, PA 19481

All rights reserved. No part of this publication may be reproduced, stored in a retrieval system, or transmitted in any form or by any means, electronic, mechanical, photocopying, recording, or otherwise, without the prior permission of the copyright owner, except for brief quotations included in a review of the book.

Library of Congress Cataloging in Publication Data

Walker, Wyatt T.
  "Somebody's calling my name."

  Includes bibliographical references and index.
  1. Afro-American music—History and criticism. 2. Gospel music—United States—History and criticism. I. Title.
ML3556.W23   783.6'7   79-14155
ISBN 0-8170-0849-7

The name JUDSON PRESS is registered as a trademark in the U.S. Patent Office.
Printed in the U.S.A. ⊕

To my wife and sweetheart of twenty-nine years, Theresa Ann, who has continually inspired me to perform difficult and worthwhile tasks and pays the price of loneliness without fretting or complaining.

Acknowledgments

I am greatly indebted to the unnamed saints of an earlier day whose heroic faith songs, coined in the midst of unspeakable cruelties, laid the foundation for a Black Sacred Music tradition. A special debt of gratitude is owed to the Irwin Sweeney-Miller Foundation that funded the Martin Luther King Program in Black Church Studies and to the Fellows and faculty whose sharing of individual and collective insights were of indispensable assistance. Two sources deserve special mention: an essay by Professor Wendel Whalum, "Black Hymnody," provided me with the "germ-idea" for this study; and *Black Song,* the monumental work of the Afro-American Spiritual, by the late John Lovell, Jr. I am grateful for both.

During the period of academic inquiry, my thesis committee was especially patient and helpful. The incisive criticism of its chairman, Dr. Henry Mitchell, made this a better work than it might have been. Professor Kofi Opoku, of the University of Ghana, and Dr. Yosef ben-Jochannan, of Cornell University, did so much to help with the understanding of African insights related to this inquiry. Very special thanks are due Dr. Thelma Adair, whose encouragement and guidance in the writing stage were of such large benefit. I appreciate deeply the hospitality and courtesy of the Yale Divinity School during a critical stage of preparing the early manuscript.

This text includes more than thirty pages of figures and illustrations directly related to the subject matter. These special devices could not have been included without the technical skill and expertise of Ray Leonardo of Leonardo Printing Company. My concept of the "Music Tree" was stylized by graphics artist Robynne W. West. There is available through the publisher a cassette tape with illustrative samples of the music described throughout. The Concert Choir of Canaan and the music staff were generous with their time and talent in the preparation of the tape.

No words are adequate to express my appreciation to those who have helped immeasurably with the tedium of authorship: Doris L. Mason, who served as a skilled and able research assistant; Mary Nunez of International House, who tenaciously handled all the details of the permission process; and Lorraine I. Springsteen, my tireless administrative assistant of fourteen years, who performed innumerable tasks so necessary to the completion of this work. The Canaan Baptist Church made the sacrifice of being without its senior minister many, many times in order that this study could proceed.

I am grateful to my colleagues in the ministry, the Reverend Elmer Williams, of Pittsburgh, Pennsylvania, and Dr. Gardner C. Taylor, of Brooklyn, New York, who read the original manuscript and offered helpful suggestions for this revision.

Author's Preface

No study covers all the ground. This inquiry is no exception. It is a general socio-historical introduction to the tradition of Black Sacred Music, the roots of which are identified with the oral tradition of West Africa. It is aimed at tracing the origin and route of the music of the Black religious experience, *in continuum,* and demonstrating its role in the development of the most powerful institution in Black life—the Black Church. It is far from being exhaustive, though it firmly establishes that a pronounced tradition exists.

This book is a revision of a doctoral thesis submitted to Colgate Rochester/Bexley Hall/Crozer in 1975. The text is considerably shorter, the documentation of sources severely limited, and the academic and theological language has been changed for lay and popular reading. Otherwise, the work remains essentially the same.

At least two areas have not been touched in the general body of the study, which does not preclude their significance or importance. One is the matter of *spirit possession.* In the Black religious experience, spirit possession is directly linked to the influence and role of music in worship. The history, need, presence, and fact of spirit possession in the Black religious experience and its relationship to music are so enormous that the author was persuaded to leave any discussion of that phenomenon to a separate inquiry.

The other area absent in discussion is *the critical role of the Pentecostal movement among Blacks,* or the "Holiness" church, in aiding the preservation of the Black Sacred Music tradition. Early in the twentieth century, as literacy among Blacks increased markedly, the introduction of hymnbook worship into the folk churches dampened the worship enthusiasm which was traditionally present. Many Black Baptists and Methodists, disenchanted with this "killing of the Spirit," flocked to the developing Pentecostal movement where spirited and lively music was encouraged and preserved. The "Holiness" churches kept alive the tradition of Black Sacred Music until latter-day Baptists and Methodists reclaimed their rejected heritage. The end result is that there is observable today a special flavor of Black Sacred Music that exists within the fellowship of Black Pentecostal Christians, with nuances that vary from denomination to denomination. Here, again, is another opportunity for a separate inquiry on the "Sacred Music of Black Pentecostalism." The family of Black Christians is indebted to our brothers and sisters in Pentecostalism who kept the fires of faith burning with song.

Thus it is, with the two exceptions noted above and the parameters established for this study, that this book proceeds in introductory fashion to explore the significance of Black folk's version of "singing the Lord's song in a strange land."

Foreword

In *"Somebody's Calling My Name,"* Dr. Wyatt Tee Walker has met a long-standing need by making available the history of Black people in America in terms of their music. Others have suggested this relationship, but memory does not recall anyone who has presented the music of American Black people as a clue to their history, or vice versa, with the thoroughness which marks *"Somebody's Calling My Name."*

Dr. Walker brings to his task an almost incomparably broad and varied background and talents every bit as diverse and rich as have been his experiences. He was a crucial part of Dr. Martin Luther King's crusade for freedom; he is a successful pastor, a preacher of notable endowments, and enjoys a talent for singing with moving power the songs of hope and sorrow about which he writes so engagingly in this volume.

One will not soon forget his meticulous tracing of the "roots" in Africa of American Black music. Dr. Walker's treatment further amplifies a reflection Booker T. Washington made about the music he heard in the "quarters" as a slave child and then as a freedman. Mr. Washington said, "People sang for hours in the evening around the fire—of war, hunting, spirits that dwell in deep woods."

Dr. Walker has given body and documentation to another comment which Booker T. Washington made about the music of his childhood. He said, "There is a difference between the music of Africa and that of her transplanted children. There is a new note in the music which had its origin in the southern plantation, and in this new note the sorrow and sufferings which came from serving in a strange land found expression." A part, perhaps the major part, of that "new note" came from the Black sufferers' particular and circumstantial viewing of the Christian faith, which was so different from what the slave masters and their religious agents had intended in the way they had presented the biblical revelation to the slave community. As this whole volume suggests, we have in the interpretation which slaves and their children gave to Christian faith a modern "glossolalia," where the masters said the Bible declared one thing and the slaves heard something far different about what the Bible declared. The owners spoke of slavery being "God-ordained"; the slaves heard, "Before I'd be a slave, I'd be buried in my grave."

Nothing has been said here of the felicity of language, the thorough documentation, the invaluable bibliography of this book. Much ought to be said of these things, since Dr. Walker has presented in these pages a rare treasury of history and reflection and he has done it with honesty and grace, which are not often seen in happy alliance.

Gardner C. Taylor
Brooklyn, New York

Contents

Introduction 1

The music of the Black religious experience is the primary root of all music born in the United States. It is an understatement to note that there is little public awareness of the crucial role of Black sacred music in the development of the broad variety of American popular music. On the strength of this fact alone, its preservation and respect should be guaranteed. However, there is greater significance to the fact that the music of Black religious life served as an indispensable support system for the establishment, growth, and continuity of the Black Church, the institution of dominant influence in the life experience of Blackamericans in the United States.

Most White Americans presume wrongly that Black people have no historic religion, music, or culture that is non-Western. Given the White versus Black syndrome of North America and the accompanying distortions of United States history, this view is understandable but remains one of grave error. The music, religion, and culture of Blackamericans are fundamentally African, both in form and substance. This book seeks to underscore the African influence in the music of the Black religious experience and critical role of that influence in the development of the Black Church. No attempt is being made to deny the Western experiences and influences in the religious life of Afro-Americans. This work will establish that the linkage between the ancestral home (Africa) of Blackamericans and their survival in the Western experience (slavery, segregation, political oppression, etc.) can be identified in an oral tradition. It was this oral and often musical tradition that survived the barbaric

Atlantic slave trade and became so pronounced in the development of Black sacred music. That same Black Church in the days of slavery, during and after Reconstruction, and in the present stands at the center of nearly every thrust for positive social change in the Black community.

A classic history lesson teaches that in many societies music is a major reservoir of a people's religion and culture. This is no less true of Afro-Americans. As mentioned earlier, the primary institution of the Black community is the Black Church. Its direct and natural antecedent is the religious music of the oral tradition. Despite the calculated and premeditated design to sever the historical umbilical cord of African heritage, the oral tradition survived—miraculously. The adaptation of the oral tradition to Western influences produced an Afro-American culture that was essential to cope with the seldom-changing oppressive Western experience. The lion's share of this hybrid culture is concentrated in the music of the Black religious experience. Thus, an examination of the beginnings and development of the music will reflect much of the response to the pain predicament of the New World African in the American experience and what impact that music has had on the development of the Black Church.

Since the Black Church is the central and dominant force in the affairs of Black people, the focus of this book is narrowed to a survey of the beginnings and development of the Black sacred music tradition. The use of that music has had an observable effect in the struggle for personal and collective liberation that can be traced to the Black Church enterprise whose basic continuity to Mother Africa is rooted in the oral tradition. It is no wonder, then, that striking parallels in the form and style of African institutions are found in the authentic Afro-American religious institutions that developed in the continental United States.

Any superficial examination will reveal that there has been an identifiable common ingredient in the Black worship style. That common ingredient has been the music of the Black Church, rooted in African musical idioms and reflecting accommodations to the "Jesus-faith." The phenomenon of Black sacred music has nourished and sustained the Black Church and undergirded its search for freedom and wholeness in the midst of oppression and injustice. Without the cohesive and integrative character of the musical tradition of the Black religious experience, the Black Church might not have become a real entity, or at best, could not have provided the operations base in the struggle for personal and political freedom in the Black community.

At this point in time, Black people are still some distance from political freedom and the absence of oppression. In fact, the conditions against which Afro-Americans have struggled so valiantly with not much more than their existentialist faith have worsened in the last few years. The one viable and independent arena which holds the potential for bringing the Black masses to the "Promised Land" of freedom and equality is the Black Church. The enabling power of the Black Church is closely tied to the retention of the historical roots which have been best preserved in its musical tradition.

There is some danger. In many instances where individual Black Churches have become imitative of White worship styles, there has been a parallel loss of freedom of expression, enthusiasm, numerical strength, and sensitivity to the gut issues that affect the Black masses. The other side of the coin is more hopeful. There is a far greater potential for a ministry of social action in those churches in which the traditional worship styles of Black folk life remain intact. The foregoing conclusion is based upon several lessons of history in Black Church life not only in the recent past but also throughout the Black people's sojourn in the "land of the free and home of the brave."

This inquiry, then, will trace the use of music in worship with a view toward demonstrating that Black people's singing was in a specific context of social circumstance. A survey of the musical content of the Black religious tradition can serve as an accurate commentary of what was happening to the Black community and its response to those conditions. Simply put, what Black people are singing religiously will provide a clue as to what is happening to them sociologically.

African Roots— 2
American Fruit

The Black Church, as the most important institution in the Black community, is the chief reservoir of Africanisms that have survived in the West. Much of the character of authentic Black religious life can be traced either directly or indirectly to Africa. The Black Church, then, is the American fruit of an African root. This study rests on that premise. It will be helpful to look for a moment at the Black Church on the North American continent and note its growth and development.

The Black Church in Historical Perspective

Any serious attempt to catalogue the growth and development of the Black community in America centers in the Black Church enterprise. Even before the erection of physical places of worship, the "invisible churches" of the Southern plantations gave cohesion and commonality to an oppressed people who had been snatched from their homeland and raped of their culture and language. These gatherings were often contrary to the pleasure of the slaveowners and had no fixed site or meeting place. Thus, the term "invisible church" is used. There were a few independent Black churches in existence in the North and fewer still in the South. However, in terms of sheer numbers, the greatest concentration of religious life and activity centered in the "invisible churches" of the Southland. It was in this setting, primarily, that the transfer of African culture took place and, as a result, Christianity was Africanized.[1]

The New World African's accommodation of the slavemaster's

religion and the retention of Africanisms produced the Jesus-faith of the antebellum slave which remains identifiable today. That Jesus-faith which was preserved for posterity in the Spirituals served to insulate the antebellum slave from the real temptation of collective suicide. The Negro Spirituals fashioned in the slave warrens of the South provided the foundation which authenticated the Black religious experience.

Following the Emancipation Proclamation, armed with their simple but profound faith that God had delivered them from "Egypt land," the ex-slaves set about the task of building their own social structures that were concentrated in the Black Church enterprise. The Black Church became the center of social intercourse and the citadel of hope against the unfulfilled promises of Emancipation. It provided the cocoon of insulation that softened the impact of the disorientation produced by America's hyprocrisy regarding freedom. The failure of the Freedmen's Bureau; the unkept promise of "forty acres and a mule";[2] the political, social, and economic disfranchisement; and the inherent ill-preparedness for urban or rural life on their own drove the newly freed slaves to internalize their meager growth and development and to focus on their religious faith. Thus, the Black Church was the proving ground for the development of leadership and literacy training.

Personal and social development took refuge under the umbrella of the Black Church. Burial societies, insurance companies, and business enterprises of every stripe frequently began in the church.[3] The free Black churches of an earlier day served as models. By the turn of the century, Black churches were playing a dominant role in the total life of freedmen as has no other institution to date.

The twentieth century saw the beginning of great emigrations to the North and Midwest. The planting of new churches began in earnest. The acquisition of real property, the establishment of church-related schools, the organization of new national conventions, and the emergence of the Black preacher as the central figure in every community, South and North, consolidated the position of the church as the center of Black energy and devotion.[4]

During World War I, great numbers of Negroes left the rural South and emigrated to the great cities of the urban North. This was induced partially by the shift in the agrarian economy and partially because of the need for manpower occasioned by the global conflict. History repeated itself following the Great Depression and the advent of World War II. The number of Blacks in the North nearly equalled those in the South.[5] Church life was preeminent in terms of numbers who were involved in Black Church activity.

Following World War II, it was easy to observe that the Black Church collectively was the largest holder of real property in the Black community.[6] The Black preacher remained as one of the most influential figures, despite the accelerating growth of a new leadership class in the oppressed community. Blacks in the entertainment world began to multiply, many of whom had sharpened their skills in church choirs or before church audiences. The election of Adam Clayton Powell, Jr., to the United States House of Representatives in 1944 underscored the latent political strength resident in Black Church life. Individual congregations swelled the ranks of Black colleges and universities by enrolling their children to prepare for the future.[7]

Then came the momentous *Brown* v. *the Board of Education* Supreme Court decision that declared in a unanimous ruling that school segregation was unconstitutional. Swift on the heels of that landmark decision in 1954 came the Montgomery bus protest, begun December 5, 1955, that ushered in more than a decade of social and civil protest unmatched since the Emancipation Proclamation. For the next dozen years, Martin Luther King, Jr., and his nonviolent followers confronted America, with a push first against blatant segregation in the South and later against the subtle and gross inequities in the North. The Southern Christian Leadership Conference (SCLC) which bore the brunt of the movement was referred to by King himself as the "home mission department of the Black Church." SCLC was made up chiefly of churches and church-linked organizations. Whatever the assessment of this era, none can deny that at the center of this struggle were the forces of the Black Church, not only as the authors of the confrontation but also as the sustaining force that provided the dynamics and vitality of the movement. The potential exists currently, provided the great resources and energy of the church are mobilized productively for the liberation struggle of Black people in contemporary America to draw its greatest help from this same Black Church.

Music and the Black Religious Tradition

The oldest and strongest (measured by their assets and numerical strength) churches in the Black community are those which might properly be called the *historic* Black churches. The added adjective narrows the province of this book and its companion assumptions to those churches whose government is ultimately in Black hands. Black congregations that are members of predominantly white denominations are understandably excluded from the purview of this inquiry. In these *historic* Black churches music plays a crucial role in the worship style and is a key mobilizing force. A common dictum in Black church circles is, "You can't organize Black folks for anything without music." A recent illustration of that dictum is the vital and essential role of music in the nonviolent movement that swept the South in the sixties. A negative aspect of that truth is obvious in the experience of the Nation of Islam (Black Muslims). No serious inroads have been made by the Muslim movement among American Blacks largely because of their failure to develop appealing music.

As music was central to West African culture, so is music central to the historic Black religious experience. This is another evidence of African survival. Music is one of the three major support systems in Black Church worship. Preaching and praying are the other two. It is difficult to say conclusively which is the most important. After the act of emancipation in 1865, preaching became central and remains so today. However, the characteristics of authentic Black preaching have been so heavily influenced by the characteristics of Black sacred music that a strong argument could be advanced to establish that singing is of equal importance. Let it suffice to submit that preaching is central, with a clear footnote that singing is a very close second. The fact is that most ministers follow a tradition of singing or attempting to sing and that any preacher who sings acceptably has a decided edge on the preacher who does not sing at all. Again, the dominance of worship time—singing versus preaching—could very well be a toss-up in almost any Black worship experience.

The music of the Black Church has a traditional and natural division: that which is performed by specialists, such as soloists, lead singers, and choirs, and that which is sung by the congregation. All told, the "music time" in most Black churches easily outstrips "preaching time."

However important or unimportant the message of the minister, the music of the Black religious tradition is a tool, a device, to raise the expectancy of the listener to a peak level in order that the maximum attention and effect are corralled for the sermon. It is not uncommon in formal and informal preaching services for there to be a special sermon solo or sermon hymn.

Black preaching, traditionally, is more auditory than literary; that is, it is aimed primarily at the ear as the route to the heart as over against being aimed at the eye as the route to the mind. You'll enjoy a sermon more if you hear it than if you read it.[8] Thus, the auditory character of Black preaching takes on a musical quality with many shades of pace and emphasis and very often with a pronounced intonation that is musical enough to have a "key." Could it be that the old-style preacher as well as the new-style preacher perceives that the rhythmic impact of music bears and shares in the message? It is well worth pondering. Consciously and/or unconsciously, the transfer is made to the preaching act. An almost identical analysis can be made of praying, the other chief support system in Black worship. Thus, in addition to the primary role that music plays in the worship of the Black religious tradition, it plays a secondary role in both preaching and praying, the other two chief support systems of the worship style under consideration.

Black Sacred Music: An Index of African Roots

The basic character of music within a congregation—Afro-American versus Euro-American—determines to a large extent the retention of African rootage. Clergy in the Black community often describe churches as being either "mass" or "class" in character. On occasions, they will concede that some churches "have a pretty good mix" but lean toward being "mass" or "class." However private this professional comment may be, it is in reality a very perceptive sociological analysis with very few exceptions.

The economic and status level of the congregation will largely determine the kind of music within a congregation. Low-income and low-status (by Western criteria) worshipers have an appetite for music that is rhythmic and emotion inducing. The worship service is enthusiastic with a relative freedom of expression, and there is no apparent hangup about singing "our music" (absence of self-rejection). Upper-income and higher-status (by Western criteria) worshipers use the value system of the dominant society and in their worship style are imitative of what is considered the "best" in white church life. The services are generally without any observable emotional expression, choir singing is minimized, and the preaching as well as the whole service are noticeably more brief. Though music is utilized to prepare for the high moment of the proclamation of the gospel, it is almost always a Euro-American anthem. In the recent past, gospel music was frequently taboo and Spirituals seldom used unless rendered as anthems. This transparent snobbery toward Black sacred music, whether intentional or not, is a form of self-rejection.

The end result is that with or without awareness, the type of church described in the first instance keeps intact the clearest evidence of Black people's ties to Africa. The church described in the second instance, perhaps unwittingly, is divorcing itself culturally from Africa and moves toward joining the culture of the dominant society, *which is the oppressor.* The religious music of Afro-Americans, past and present, is geared to liberation themes. The music of Euro-American churches was not created in the social context of resistance to racism and oppression. It is patently clear that people at worship should be singing the music that relates directly to their social context. The social context of Black people is the need for liberation from racism and oppression.

If Black people are to pursue the most direct route to liberation via religion, there is a need for them to embrace the music which in large measure has demonstrated its relevance and usefulness in resisting racism and oppression. The Black Church, then, as the chief reservoir of Black sacred music, holds a vast potential for a ministry of social change at both the personal and collective levels. Collective liberation can only follow personal liberation.

The argument set forth above has dealt with the extreme poles in question for the sake of analysis. This approach is not intended to suggest that there is no middle ground. The middle ground, though present, is severely limited. However, a summary comment is in order. The Black Church of the future ideally should have the best of both the "mass" and the "class" churches. There are too few models on the contemporary scene, but they do exist. Under enlightened leadership, there are congregations who have gathered the skills and resources of the larger community without sacrificing the tradition of Blackness in worship. The end product is a worship experience that is both intellectually challenging and emotionally satisfying. That bicultural worship style induces a broad arena of interests in life-style that includes the vital life concerns, such as housing, increased employment opportunities, federal credit unions, and voter registration.

Roots and Liberation

If indeed the music in a Black congregation is an accurate index of African rootage, then a companion truth follows. It is the other side of the same coin. The overt, spirit-filled quality or style of worship will be in direct proportion to the retention of the African rootage mentioned above.

The flavor of worship in the dominant white Protestant churches of America can be described charitably as *restrained.* Only in the so-called sect religions and flowering Pentacostalism is there any semblance of the enthusiasm in worship found among the mass-oriented churches in the Black community. The restraint may be attributable to the exaggerated rationality of Western society which has programmed many Americans to believe that to be emotional is to be unintellectual. Following the Great Awakening under Jonathan Edwards and the Second Awakening early in the nineteenth century, the worship services in white churches began to be drained of the spirit and enthusiasm that were once the earmark of the frontier religion. The spirit of intellectualism contributed to the rising secularism in America and the downgrading of emotion. It is understandable, then, that Black congregations that were to become imitative of White worship styles did so with a parallel loss of enthusiasm and spirited worship so native and natural to their beginnings. As the style of worship changed, so did the style and character of music, which so heavily influences the style of worship—White or Black. Wherever Black congregations were resistant to White influences, the music of the forefathers remained intact, and the link to Mother Africa was retained.

The phenomenon of overt enthusiasm in worship has not been without Western input. The revivalism of Dwight Moody and Ira Sankey with its livelier music provided some of the raw materials with which the Gospel era of Black sacred music developed.

The music of the Black religious tradition is undeniably emotion evoking, all the way from the original field songs of faith to modern Gospel. It follows, then, that to the degree that Afro-American music is utilized in worship, the emotional content of the service will be high; to the degree that Euro-American music is utilized, the emotional content of the service will be low.

Given both sides of the coin, wherever African rootage remains intact or is rediscovered, there is a greater *potential* for a ministry of social change. This conclusion is carefully worded. It ends with, "there is a greater potential for a ministry of social change." The elimination of the music of the Black religious tradition from worship leaves only the alternative of moving toward the Euro-American style of worship. This style is imitative of the dominant society and identifies with that which has no abiding interest and support for liberation of the oppressed. If this seems a harsh and severe judgment of white churches in the land, consider the historical track record. White churches have gone along with the program of white America, whatever it was—slavery, segregation, discrimination, with few notable exceptions. There has always been within white Christianity, however, a "remnant" of the faithful. The monumental task of educating the freedmen would have faltered disastrously had there not been committed teachers of the Christian faith who absorbed painful indignities and accepted little pay for their selfless work. In every period of unusual stress in the life of the Black community, this "remnant" has made its presence felt as, for example, in the Underground Railroad and in Birmingham, 1963.

The presence of the music of the Black religious tradition has served as a device to fire and fuel most of the efforts, large and small, for the liberation of the oppressed—personally and collectively. Stated another way, it has been the churches peopled with the masses which have retained the music and worship style that is identifiably Africa linked and which have been in the forefront of much of the struggle for liberation.

Since "class" churches are fewer in number and smaller statistically in population, and since "mass" churches are far more numerous and, as the name tag suggests, have many more people, the *greater potential* lies with the "mass" churches.

The Oral Tradition **3**
Sails West

People spoke before they wrote. The Scriptures, both Old and New Testaments, are products of oral transmission. In the African experience, oral transmission is of long duration despite the invention of the printing press at Gutenberg. The history, culture, and religion of Africa have been preserved by the telling and retelling of its lore from one generation to another for hundreds of years. Thus, it is historically accurate and acceptable to speak of Africa in a context of an oral tradition.[1] The oral tradition can be defined as the transmission by word of mouth through ceremony, song, drum, and folk wisdom of the mores, customs, and religious rites of African peoples that persisted through the Atlantic slave trade and influenced the worship forms and patterns of Afro-Americans.

The Oral Tradition in North America
The conventional view of the enslaved Africans is that they came to these shores heathen and primitive.[2] What developed in and around them, by design or providence, "civilized" them. Only in recent years, with the rise of interest in Africa, has the general public had available the great wealth of documentary evidence that refutes altogether that persistent conventional view. C. L. R. James, celebrated Howard University professor and chronicler of Afro-American history, speaks incisively to this issue. The New World African ". . . brought with him the content of his mind, his memory. He thought in the logic and the language of his people. . . . He valued that which his previous life had taught him to value. . . ."[3]

Another part of the conventional view is the implicit and sometimes explicit assertion that the Africans accepted slavery willingly. Just the opposite was true. Indigenous Africans, from wherever they came, resisted slavery at every turn.[4] Suicide was not uncommon even before they boarded the ships used to transport them to the New World. Slavery was such an assault on their personhood that some sank into deep melancholia or infantilism, refusing to eat or drink, and died en route. Others chose to perish in the dark waters of the Atlantic, shouting glad farewells as they sank. Numerous accounts tell of mass suicides by drowning at ports of entry and desperate dashes for freedom that ended more often in death than escape.[5]

The African hostility to slavery was compounded by the cruelties of the Middle Passage, the White faces in charge, and the long sea voyage that physically removed Africans from all that was familiar and friendly. In spite of the systemic brutality of the slave trade, the social consciousness of these indigenous Africans was not destroyed. John Blassingame notes the emotional and psychological hardiness of these uprooted Africans as evidenced by their tenacious hold, through memory alone, on the cultural determinants of their own status.[6] This hold is evident in the feeble attempts to retain some of that which had given them wholeness in Africa—remnants of traditional African religion, preserved in its native instrumentality, the oral tradition.

John Lovell, Jr., in an early essay that details the origin and development of the Negro folk spiritual, underscores the African's universal resistance to slavery by noting not only the physical revolts but, more importantly, the mental revolts also. "Uprising slaves were shot or hanged and that was the end of them physically; but the mind of the slave seethed ceaselessly, and was a powerful factor in the abolition movement."[7]

To understand the depth and deep-rootedness of the oral tradition, one must appreciate several facts about African life and culture that not only antedate the Atlantic slave traffic but are also apparent today. It has been mentioned earlier that African history has been preserved in its music. Troubadours, storytellers, and *griots* (official village historians) have been the history keepers.

Within the context of the holistic theological systems of Africa, all life is manifestly religious. The events of life—birth, death, puberty, fertility, harvest, famine, marriage, tragedy—have religious rites that give expression to the event. In the absence of any prescribed written formula as to what is done and when, the music and the companion ceremony have been the key to the orchestration of events and the primary preservative ingredient of tradition. There is no gainsaying, then, the importance and dominance of music in the life of the indigenous African, past or present. How natural, then, in the face of the admittedly bestial slave trade that the uprooted forebears of Blackamericans would retain at least the musical forms of their culture in a desperate attempt to escape total dehumanization! The widespread practice of separating slaves on the basis of geographical origins and language was another major factor that contributed to the survival of the musical idiom and rhythm forms. Considerable care was taken to keep sizable numbers of Africans with a common tongue separate. The obvious purpose was to minimize the chance of rebellion or escape. With no common tongue, the musical expression was reduced to chants and moans on the rhythm forms and in the musical idioms that survived. As the slaves learned the language of the masters, their verbal commonality became most pronounced in the music that developed in the context of slavery.

The rhythm forms and musical idioms were kept alive through the desperate need of the Africans for humanness, which the slave system forcibly stripped from them. It was a vital link to their sense of being. Throughout the pain of the Middle Passage and their introduction into the Caribbean, they kept alive snatches of what they could remember from the Mother Country.

In the Caribbean, African survivals remained more pronounced due to the presence of the drum. However, African survivals were hard pressed on the North American continent due to the severe restrictions on the use of the drum and other instruments throughout the slave period. Ortiz Walton comments on this fact and notes the ingenious substitution by the slaves of the handclap and foot pat in place of the drum.[8] Despite the outlawing of the slave trade in 1807, a sizable and continuing flow of contraband slaves continued until 1860.[9] This continuing influx of new Africans reinforced the African survivals that influenced the shape and style of the religious life of the antebellum slave society.

The transference of the character and values of the oral tradition was the enabling force in the development of the Jesus-faith that became so crucial in the life of the antebellum slave community. Without the instrumentality of the oral tradition, the master's religion could never have served as the "cover" for the slave people's unquenched thirst for freedom. All of the above was begun, developed, and preserved in the musical expression of the slave community.

The Oral Tradition and the Invisible Church

In many quarters of American religious life today, it is generally assumed that the Black religious experience has its organic origin in White religious life. That assumption is questionable in light of the ambivalence exhibited by the planters in their attitude toward regular formal religious instructions and the prospect of what might occur if the slaves became Christian. Even when the first wave of the Great Awakening touched the plantations of the South, the planters were dubious as to whether the acceptance of religion on the part of the slaves would be good or bad in the long run. Where permission to assemble under tight monitoring was granted, the proclamation of the gospel was just as tightly monitored as the assembly itself. C. E. Lincoln's blistering essay reports that the celebrated Cotton Mather arranged for the religious instruction of slaves but was prudent that such instruction did not conflict with work schedules and that sufficient personnel were present to thwart any plan of rebellion or escape.[10] Care was taken in most instances to provide only a slave-master's view of sound biblical doctrine—that of *maintaining slavery!*

There were some sparse efforts made by the planters to provide formal religious instruction for their chattel. Even so, there is adequate evidence that those of the slave community were well aware that their evangelization was being used to keep the noose of slavery tight. The separate seats at worship and the diluted form of the "Good News" that emphasized "obedience to your master" and encouraged servile docility were rejected. Even though the slaves did not (perhaps could not) absent themselves from the master's catechism classes, Bible reading, and the like, there spread across the Southland the steady development of what is now termed the "invisible church." The slaves formulated new ideas and practices on their own and specifically colored their religious principles with a pronounced longing for freedom. The meetings in the brush arbor and praise houses were filled with ecstatic singing that climaxed in a veritable frenzy of emotion.[11] They were charged with the hope of freedom through faith in "sweet Jesus."

The "invisible church" consisted of services conducted among slaves, illegally in many instances, where the worship took on an altogether different tone from the tone in those services held under the auspices of the plantation owners. They met from place to place on individual plantations and sometimes on adjoining or nearby plantations out of earshot of the master's "big house." This "invisible church" was a direct response to the hypocrisy of the owner's religious faith and practice. The double meaning of the words of the faith songs evidenced the irony and resentment present. The Spiritual verse "Ev'rybody talkin' 'bout heab'n ain't goin' dere" is just one example.[12]

The meetings of the "invisible church" could not have proceeded without the instrumentality of the oral tradition. The sheer force of circumstance required the slaves to "adopt" the language of the master. This, coupled with the Bible narratives they picked up from religious practice around them (Bible reading and segregated worship services) provided the slaves with the raw material to fashion their own concept of God's providence and concern in the hellish condition of servitude. The dialect English words transposed into the context of religious hope provided a universal verbal commonality that heretofore was unparalleled. Where interplantation visits were allowed or *managed,* the transfers and exchange of new songs became possible with the verbal commonality necessary to the slave community. Wherever the slaves met, conventionally or unconventionally, the exchange inevitably took place. By the beginning of the nineteenth century, a sizable body of musical faith-literature had developed in the slave community through the instrumentality of the oral tradition. In fact, many of the hymns of Isaac Watts learned by rote were making the rounds of plantations in an adapted form unique to the antebellum slave society.[13] Frequently, snatches of verse lifted directly from hymns of Euro-American authorship were incorporated into the Spiritual music form that had developed as an integral part of worship in these "invisible churches." In the preliterate era of slavery, the fuel of the "invisible church" was the musical expression constantly fed by the oral tradition mentioned earlier. The religious expression of Black people could not have developed or survived without constant reinforcement of this oral tradition.

There remains still another aspect of the oral tradition's role in the life of the slave. It is to be found in the double meaning of the faith songs. The reader must keep in mind that the "invisible church" was the forum of all Black hopes and aspiration for justice and freedom. The most dangerous of these hopes and aspiration was escape via the Underground Railroad run by abolitionist "stationmasters" and Black "conductors and trainmen." The most famous of this network was the ex-slave Harriet Tubman. The "invisible church" was the Black grapevine of this network, and often the music was used as the code and signal of movement. Hence, the double meaning of the Spirituals. An amplified discussion will be found in the next chapter, but mention should be made here in order to make full circle of those elements that contributed to the development of the "invisible church," whose chief instrumentality was the oral tradition. There is no intent to make a case that the double meaning was apart and separate from the basic character of the spirituals; this aspect is noted here only for the sake of analysis. John Lovell, in discussing the social impact of the Spiritual, lists three elements as the *leit motif* of most Spirituals. They are, first, "the Negro's obsession for freedom," second, "the slave's desire for justice . . . upon his betrayers," and, third, "the strategy . . . to gain an eminent future." [14] What more logical forum than the "invisible church" existed for the transmission of any and all information that had to do with the possibility of escape? When the word was given, through song, that a section of the Underground Railroad was "passing through," at the risk of life and limb those who dared would make their bid for freedom. As the train moved northward, its passage was noted from farm to farm, county to county, and state to state via the double meaning of an oral tradition in song.

The slave society, in covert form, encouched its criticism of slavery in symbolic language at many points. With the increased activity of the Underground Railroad, it was fairly common that the faith songs gave instructions for "catching the train to freedom." In effect, they were not only the words of a faith language resisting the brutal assault of slavery on their personhood, but songs were also *political* language at points, dealing with escape from the system itself. The oral tradition was, then, the *pièce de résistance* when the religious music was utilized. Thus, the oral tradition as a device was indispensable to the development and operation of the "invisible church" and the several purposes which that church served within the slave community—including the logistics for escape to the North and Canada.

The Oral Tradition and the Negro Spiritual

Some brief comment needs to be made here about the Negro Spiritual because of its connection to the oral tradition and its role in the development of the "invisible church." A broader exposition on the Spiritual follows in the next chapter.

It was important to the development of the slave community's sense of group solidarity that they create a music form in which they could all participate.[15] Equally important, if not more important, was the message carried by the music form. The message, universally, was the distaste for the slave system, and it found expression in the secular as well as the sacred folk music of the era.[16] Very often, the two were intertwined with the common theme of antislavery sentiment. The primary forum for the expression of this sentiment was the "invisible church" discussed above.

There is little doubt that the Spiritual and the family of music of which it is a part are genuine folk music. The very use of the nomenclature suggests strongly in its development that its end product, by definition, would reflect its cohesive and integrative influence on the slave community. Folk music, both old and contemporary, is representative of the people's ancient traditions as indicators of their current tastes. Lovell makes the case conclusively that the Spiritual is folk music. Thus, its existence proves that this body of literature spoke for the slave community and expressed its universal disenchantment with the slave system, with the injustices and the inhumanity that ripped families apart and inflicted torment upon its victims. Crucial to understanding the folk character of the testimony of the Spirituals is to recognize that it is internal testimony. The perception of the Spirituals is a view from the inside out—as the slaves viewed slavery themselves and not as historians and observers made notes outside of slavery. In a common voice, through the Spirituals they spoke of hope for deliverance, and unlike Israel of old, they gladly sang the Lord's song in a strange land.

The Spirituals do not always speak directly to the slave system, though the veiled hope for the Promised Land was always present. Songs of sorrow and hope are more dominant, but it must be remembered that their point of departure was the loosing of the chains of slavery in this world or the next, but preferably this world. Nearly all the Spirituals are derivatives of biblical themes, but heavy emphasis fell upon those themes where by supernatural means God delivered the faithful from impossible circumstances. Wendel Whalum underscores the biblical basis of the Spiritual in an essay on Black hymnody. "The *Bible*, more than any other one source, provided the textual material for the religious music which is at the base of a consideration of Black hymnody." [17] Whalum asserts that in addition to music being expressive of the gamut of human experience, the constant theme here was freedom. [18]

The common thread and theme of Spiritual music were "De udder worl' is not like dis." Release and freedom, physical and spiritual, were the slave's uppermost concern. It is difficult to deny that without the faith transmitted via the means of the common music vehicle (the Spirituals), the New World Africans might not have developed the spiritual resiliency to endure what they had to endure. In the community of suffering, the slaves found life bearable through the religious faith instilled in the folk community by singing the language of faith—the Spirituals.

The question might be raised, "Why was music the vehicle?" Primarily, music was (is) culturally natural to indigenous Africans. Lovell's comment in this regard is specific.

> Music is intimately connected with African custom and practice. It is the foremost Negro social art, the right hand, says Hichens of the native physiology. He is born, named, initiated into manhood, warriored, armed, housed, betrothed, wedded, buried—to music. After he dies his spirit is invoked or appeased through music. [19]

Secondarily, in many instances the slaves were required by the planters to sing in order to increase work productivity and to establish the locus of the slaves. [20] Add to that the need for the slaves to communicate when conversation was forbidden. The social

context of the music was slavery; the hope was freedom; music was
the vehicle for the transmission of that hope; and the oral tradition
was the dynamic that allowed the music to live.

FIGURE 1
POPULATION TABLE[21]
1619–1860
(Continental U.S.A.)

Year	Slave	Free	% Free
1619	20	0	0
1700	27,817	(undetermined)	—
1730	91,021	(undetermined)	—
1750	236,420	c. 25,000	11
1790	697,624	59,557	9
1810	1,191,362	186,448	18
1840	2,487,355	386,293	17
1860	3,953,760	488,070	14

"Hush! Somebody's 4 Calling My Name!"

The Afro-American Spiritual

The oral tradition that survived the horrors of the Middle Passage and the bestiality of the American slave system persisted and contributed largely to an ever-widening circle of musical expression. A large part of that expression is the primary focus of this book— *Black sacred music.*

The members of the antebellum slave community were, for the most part, totally illiterate and thus exhibited complete dependence on oral transmission for news and communication of any kind. Roach noted this critical fact:

> The method of oral tradition was greatly responsible for the maintenance of the samples of African heritage which miraculously survived the centuries. Because of the illiteracy of most Blacks (at least in the English language) and because of the diversity of African languages, a process of rote teaching was instrumental in sustaining the legends and music of old Africa. Although many Africans had composed their own symbols to represent language sounds, the oral tradition was still by far the most common practice in Africa for decades, and remained the most effective method of reaching the thousands of slaves in America.[1]

Because of the stringent codes which buttressed the slave system, musical expression developed as the chief means of covert communication among the slaves.

The question might be raised, "What about the influences of free Blacks?" The answer to that question must be taken in accurate historical perspective. Figure 1 illustrates that no sizable number of Blacks, slave or free, inhabited the North American continent until

FIGURE 2

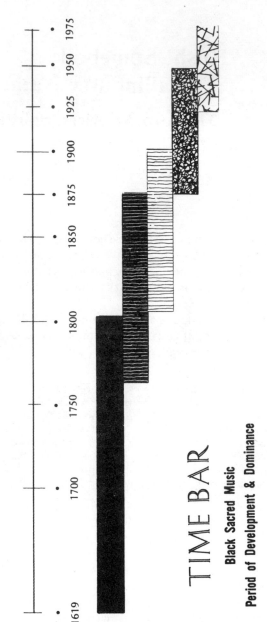

TIME BAR

Black Sacred Music

Period of Development & Dominance

1619 1700 1750 1800 1850 1875 1900 1925 1950 1975

SLAVES UTTERANCES/Moans, Chants, Cries for Deliverance

SPIRITUALS/Faith-Songs, Sorrow Songs, Plantation Hymns, etc.

METER MUSIC/Watts, Wesley, Sankey et al.

HYMNS OF IMPROVISATION/Euro-American hymns with "beat"

GOSPEL MUSIC/Music of Hard Times (Cross fertilization with secular)

well after 1700. The other figures demonstrate that the number of Black free men and women was far disproportionate to those enslaved, and as the number of slaves increased numerically, the percentage of free men and women decreased!

First, it must be clearly understood that solely on the basis of numbers, the predominant amount of religious life and practice among Blacks was in the slave circumstance. Second, the few free or independent Black churches that had been established prior to the Emancipation Proclamation and the precious few Blacks who held membership in White churches had only a negligible impact on the religious tradition under scrutiny. When one talks about a Black religious tradition, musical or otherwise, one presumes, among other things, widespread and general practice. The scarcity of influence of free Black churches in this regard is obvious, as reflected in the table.

Black sacred music began, grew, developed, and expanded in the "invisible church" of the antebellum slave society. This disclaimer is crucial in order to understand that those of the slave community came by the influence of the Watts hymns *while* they were developing their own music.[2] The slaves' use and development of the Spiritual form produced the New World Africans' unique imprint on the meter music that came to ascendancy in the latter days of slavery. This book will study the musical expression of the Black religious tradition with a view toward identifying the African influences that contributed to its development and will note how the oral tradition contributed to that development and continues to influence the music of the Black religious experience today.

In the preceding chapter, heavy emphasis was laid upon the transfer of African influences onto the religious music developed by the slaves through the instrumentality of the West African oral tradition. That emphasis was designed to establish that the ground root of the Black religious experience is that undeniable musical art form commonly called "the Spiritual."

In the line of progression from African survivals—chants, moans, utterances—it is probable that the first music might well have been work and game songs. If, as the table indicates, no sizable number of Africans inhabited the continental U.S. until after 1700, it follows that some lapse of time was necessarily required to develop music of any kind. The process of adaptation of the religious impulse which was brought with the slave from Africa and the accommodation necessary to the Jesus-faith took some time.

The best estimate of the earliest appearances of the Spiritual, as we know it, is 1760.[3] Surely the slaves were singing and creating the early folk music of America previous to this date. However, it must be made clear, also, that the first *religious* music of the antebellum slaves was the "Spiritual" or "Sorrow Songs."[4] For this writer and many specialists in the field, no sharp distinction is made between the "Sorrow Songs" and the great body of music called "Spirituals." There are a few experts who make that distinction, and none so strongly as Zora Neale Hurston.[5]

In summary, the first evidence of the music coined in the antebellum slave community was the development of the "Sorrow Songs," or "Spirituals." Though antedated by work and game songs, the social context of both them and the Spirituals created generally a parallel development of both strains. This produced, understandably, a pronounced similarity of form and rhythm. It is not uncommon to find religious songs with touches of humor and work and play songs with religious references.

The Spirituals were created and refined by the slaves themselves as religious and social statements about the context of their lives. The broad use of the Spiritual was increased through Blacks evangelizing one another. The rise of Methodism and the inevitable contact with the masters of the plantation system introduced the slaves to the Watts hymns which they appropriated and stamped with their special genius and flavor.

In this chapter a brief examination will be made first of the social and political context of slavery, then the social statement or response reflected in the general period of development (1760–1865), and finally a profile of the music with some illustrations appended. This schema will serve as the general outline for the several types of music that developed in the Black religious tradition and are discussed in the chapters that follow.

The types chosen as samples of Black sacred music are not exhaustive nor by any means arbitrary. An attempt has been made to lift up those types that are easiest to identify and can be fixed loosely in time periods of major impact and importance to the community in whose loins this music still lives. Special attention is given to the

FIGURE 3

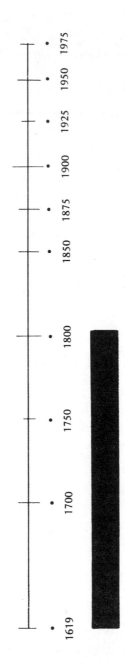

1619 1700 1750 1800 1850 1875 1900 1925 1950 1975

TIME BAR

Black Sacred Music

Period of Development & Dominance

 SLAVES UTTERANCES/Moans, Chants, Cries for Deliverance

FIGURE 4

TIME BAR

Black Sacred Music

Period of Development & Dominance

 SLAVES UTTERANCES/Moans, Chants, Cries for Deliverance

SPIRITUALS/Faith-Songs, Sorrow Songs, Plantation Hymns, etc.

1619   1700   1750   1800   1850   1875   1900   1925   1950   1975

influences that contributed to the period of a particular type of music's ascendancy.

The Period of Slavery—1619–1865

The Spirituals are the heart music of all other American music. They are the taproot of the musical expression of the Black religious experience. Some specialists dicker about the accuracy of calling the music spawned in pre-Civil War days "Spirituals." They are called by many names, depending largely upon who is the author of the nomenclature. Though they have been referred to variously as jubilee, minstrel, religious, slave, or folk songs, the Spirituals have traditionally been an umbrella for many cries and expressions of the human spirit in bondage. *In bondage!* That phrase is of paramount importance. The political and social significance of the Spiritual will be obscured if one loses sight of the fact that the Spirituals were born in slavery. It will be both helpful and instructive to take a look at the conditions imposed upon the New World African who came to these shores between 1619 and 1860. Those conditions, for the most part, have been studiously concealed and ignored in this republic until recent days.

In the late spring of 1974, Dean Morton of the Cathedral of Saint John the Divine (Episcopal, New York) served as convener of an impressive gathering of scholars and theologians. The three-day conference was called *Auschwitz* and was purported to have as one of its goals "to sensitize the American public under thirty" to the horror of the six million Jews destroyed in the Nazi holocaust under Hitler. Afro-Americans should demand equal time. Few Americans, *over* or *under* thirty, have any real insight into the reality of what it meant to be a slave in America between the day that Dutch sloop anchored in Jamestown and the misfortunes of the Civil War that forced Lincoln to sign the Emancipation Proclamation. Unconscionable as was the slaughter of six million Jews with barely an outcry from the Euro-American community of nations, how much more unconscionable the genocide hidden and concealed in this land! By conservative estimate, upward of fourteen million Africans were imported into the Americas during the Atlantic slave trade. For every African that reached these shores alive, four died in the machinery of slavery at one end or the other of the traffic or in the dreadful Middle Passage.

That's at least sixty million people lost from West Africa in less than four hundred years—genocide on a scale unmatched in recorded history.[6] A conference on the Middle Passage is long overdue!

If the genocide of the slave traffic was not enough to inflict upon a people, add to their surviving posterity in the New World, according to historian Kenneth Stampp, "a social system as coercive as any yet known erected on a foundation of the most implacable race-consciousness yet observed in virtually any society."[7]

In the early days of slavery, the race of a slave was incidental in the New World. It was not long before the colonists discovered that the Indian was unsuited to slavery and the supply of white slaves was very limited. Blacks were elected unanimously. In a few decades the weight of law was added to the degradation of enslaved Blacks so that by 1667, even religion was overruled, and the basis of servitude was shifted totally to race.

During the next thirty years, in the plantation colonies laws were enacted that made color the mark of servitude. It became illegal to permit a black slave to read or write, and no more than five slaves could ever assemble without the presence of a white man. Signed passes were the prerequisite for any movement of slaves beyond their own quarters. By 1700, American slavery had developed all the legal apparatus that was to make it "the most oppressive form of slavery the world has ever known."[8]

In spite of specious laws and the infamous Black Codes that were so restrictive to the sociality of slaves, some sense of family and community evolved.[9] It is to the everlasting glory and honor of Black people that under such systemic harsh treatment they survived at all and, beyond that survival, gave birth to America's most authentic music in the veritable hell of the American slave system. That music played a crucial role in buttressing the fragile network of the family and slave community. James Weldon Johnson catches the terror of the day in the second stanza of the Negro National Anthem:

> Stony the road we trod;
> Bitter the chastening rod
> Felt in the day when hope unborn had died. . . .

The recent cliometric studies (application of mathematical and statistical methods) of the American slave system have provided valuable insights about the material aspects of slavery. Some long-held views have been considerably altered.[10] However, the cliometricians themselves confess the limitation of their methods:

> And, while the cliometricians have been able to construct reasonably reliable indexes of the material level at which blacks lived under slavery, *it has been impossible,* thus far, to devise a meaningful index of the effect of slavery on the personality or psychology of blacks [author's italics].[11]

One of the most interesting conclusions drawn by the cliometric studies has to do with a much higher incidence of family life among slaves than previously supposed. A rather persuasive argument is set forth that describes the function of the slave family within the slave system. It is evident that if family life among the slaves was permitted or encouraged, the slave family existed primarily for the utilitarian purpose of the slave economy.[12] There is little evidence that the morality or goodwill of the planters played an appreciable role in this regard. Whatever resultant positive ends developed from this contrived economic unit of slavery were due to the humanity of the slaves themselves.

The historical and mythical African past was all but destroyed by slavery. There remained one instrumentality that slavery could not destroy—the oral tradition of the slaves' African heritage. And where better to ply that instrumentality than in the only thing left—music! That music, in turn, became the medium of all the yearning for peace and freedom. That which the slaves dared not breathe in public word they disguised in song and thereby kept a vital part of their humanity intact and their hope alive. Thus was fashioned the religious music of the antebellum slave.

Social Significance of the Spiritual

The most crucial aspect of social change and development for the New World Africans was the resistance they demonstrated to total dehumanization. The syncretized religion that they developed was the focus of that resistance. It surfaced in the music of the antebellum slave period and was carried out by the instrumentality of the oral tradition that survived the horrendous Atlantic slave trade. Wendel Whalum, a contemporary authority on the Afro-American Spiritual, notes that despite the Spiritual being rooted in a Black life-style that was desperately trying to cope with poor social conditions, there was never acceptance of those poor conditions because hope was always the Spiritual's central theme.[13]

When one considers the hostile environment in which Spirituals were born and developed, it is easily understood why the primary representation of the Spiritual must be seen as the implicit tenacious insistence on the slaves' humanity. The matter of self-image is crucial to an oppressed people, individually and collectively. The deposit of the preliterate slaves' creative energy into the development of this marvelous mine of music, more than anything else, affirmed their humanity. With their humanity intact, the slaves were better fortified to endure what they had to endure in the midst of the slave and caste system in America.

Another pronounced aspect of social significance of the Spiritual music is the recurring theme of the hope and confidence of liberation. The religious form of the Black sacred folk song may induce the naive and uninformed to believe that the hope for "Canaan" or the "Promised Land" was only resignation to a release by death. There is solid evidence that interspersed in the biblical language was the code meaning with specific reference to the Underground Railroad and the route and risk of the freedom trail. The monumental work of John Lovell referred to earlier, *Black Song: The Forge and the Flame,* contains an entire section (not chapter) entitled "The Slave Sings Free" which details carefully all the evidences of the enslaved African's concern with this world and its conditions as well as the sure judgment of the oppressors in the next world. Chapter 17 of that book, "Radical Change in the Existing Order of Things," is of special import in this regard.

A recent volume, *Black American Music: Past and Present,* authored by Hildred Roach, underscores the detail with which the body of Spirituals mirrored the social context in which they grew and developed. Roach observes the multiple function of the Spiritual form. Not only were they religious, but they also served additionally to teach, gossip, scold, and were used in the search for freedom. The Spiritual was an indispensible device of recreation and information within the slave community.[14]

From a sociological point of view, perhaps the primary contribution of the Spirituals to the slave community was the cohesive influence they had upon the "invisible church" and the general populace of the slave quarters. It was the music of the slaves more than anything else that gave them a sense of community. Everyone could participate, and the Spiritual form and performance were nonexclusionary, as Whalum notes: "If a member of the group could not sing, he could pat his foot; if he could not pat, he could sway his head; and if he could not do this, he could witness."[15]

Lovell has the fullest and best organized exposition this writer has come across that details precisely how the music of the Spirituals choreographed the dynamics of the slave community. The purposes of the Spiritual are listed in summary form:

1. To give the community a true, valid, and useful song
2. To keep the community invigorated
3. To inspire the uninspired individual
4. To enable the group to face its problems
5. To comment on the slave situation
6. To stir each member to personal solutions and to a sense of belonging in the midst of a confusing and terrifying world
7. To provide a code language for emergency use[16]

It takes very little deduction in light of the list above to understand that the Spiritual music of this era was the major support system of the "invisible church." Music was far more important than preaching as we know it today. As one studies the route of development of Black sacred music of the oral tradition, it is fairly reasonable to conclude that the singing of these songs antedated preaching.[17] The social context of the slave and the fixed dates of the beginnings of these songs are much earlier than the Black preaching tradition. If this conjecture is sound, the musical style and tonality of Black preaching have been influenced more by music than vice versa.

One other word might be added under this section that underscores the social significance of the Spiritual. The timeless quality of the Spiritual is of social significance also. Who has said it better than the matchless W. E. B. Du Bois?

And so by fateful chance the Negro folk-song—the rhythmic cry of the slave—stands to-day not simply as the sole American music, but as the most beautiful expression of human experience born this side [of] the seas. It has been neglected, it has been, and is, half despised, and above all it has been persistently mistaken and misunderstood; but notwithstanding, it still remains as the singular spiritual heritage of the nation and the greatest gift of the Negro people.[18]

The Spiritual is of social significance not only because of the religious message it bears but also because of its widespread musical influence. Despite the fact that the creation of Spirituals ended shortly after the Emancipation Proclamation, their influence in the family of Black music continued. The Afro-American Spiritual has colored all the forms of Black sacred music, and almost every single form of American popular music has felt its influence either directly or indirectly. Among the American music art forms that the Spiritual counts as its heirs are minstrel songs, jazz, blues, ragtime, gospel, and "soul" music.

Profile of the Spiritual

There is preponderant evidence that the music of present-day Blackamericans contains a circuitous yet direct link to Mother Africa. The initial link in that chain in North America is the Black tradition of sacred song exhibited most in what John Lovell terms the Afro-American Spiritual. Wherever the Africans and their progeny touched New World shores, no matter what the condition of their existence, they maintained their musical identity. Maud Cuney Hare is explicit in identifying the "rhythmic relationship and melodic similarity" between music indigenous to Africa and the folk song of American Blacks.[19] W. E. B. Du Bois in that unforgettable and prophetic essay, "Of the Sorrow Songs," the concluding narrative of *The Souls of Black Folk,* tells of a native African hymn passed down through his family for two hundred years with the African tongue intact.[20] Du Bois marveled that it was so similar in rhythm, tone, and texture to the sorrow songs of which he wrote. Lovell says strongly that the principles and practices of holistic religion, "exerted daily generation after generation," could not be forgotten or wiped out by slavery.[21] Thus the persistence of the transported African's musical identity.

Melville Herskovits, in his classic *Myth of the Negro Past,* conclusively establishes the fact of African survivals in the New World.[22] In technical musical terms, he traces the antiphonal and responsorial character in African music directly to these shores. Herskovits concedes that there are American influences but that the

African elements are dominant. The evidence of transfer from Africa to America in musical style and rhythm forms is specific and overwhelming in the literature of scholars with impeccable credentials.[23] African specialists in the field, such as Ballanta Taylor and Alakija, report that melodies identical to those still sung in the South are extant in Africa today.[24] Add to those experts already noted the list of foreign researchers cited by Lovell who hold the view of the "African connection," such as Swami Parampanthi, J. Stanislaz, and Frederika Bremer. Hildred Roach contends that in spite of the European influences present in African American music, Africa remained the most important source of originality for Blacks in their musical expression. Miss Roach makes a broader point than this discussion requires. Not only is the Spiritual linked to Africa, but also much of the music America calls its own is Africa linked! Roach's conclusion is unarguable: "The definition of African music represented the core of Black music in America."[25]

Despite the heterogeneity of the West and central African nations from which the slaves came, the music was amazingly homogeneous. John Rublowsky, in his perceptive volume *Black Music in America,* lists the principal characteristics of West African music as being: (1) spontaneous creation, (2) melody, (3) harmony, (4) rhythm, and (5) the means of communication (based upon the musical elements of rhythm and melody).[26]

Rublowsky describes the journey of this music from Africa to America:

> This music and tradition came to America in the holds of the slave ships, along with the forcibly transported Africans. It was a rich tradition, sophisticated and highly developed, with unique concepts of sound and melody, of rhythm and the use of the voice.[27]

It is easy to see the evidence of the parallels in the music of Africa and the music we know as the Afro-American Spirituals.

Some mention must be made of the process of evolution of this musical literature. These immigrants of coercion became musical catalysts, borrowing at times from the music around them. The end product was enriched by their African past and what they remembered from the oral tradition of West Africa which became the chief instrument of their survival. The African input was constantly reinforced by the influx of contraband slave traffic that persisted until 1860.[28]

Howard Thurman suggests that there were three main sources of material (lyric) that were utilized in the slave warrens to create this spiritual testimony of the New World Africans' unflinching faith that they, too, were children of God: the Bible, the world of nature, and the personal experience of religion.[29]

It is apparent, then, that the Spiritual was fashioned from a variety of sources, and its form was influenced by a variety of needs. Thus, the earliest Black sacred oral literature reflects an umbrella use and function. The Spiritual was a device for such a variety of purposes that different experts have underscored different emphases as to what the specific or dominant thrusts were intended to be by the originators of the Spirituals. The late Miles Mark Fisher, a Baptist clergyman of Durham, North Carolina, concluded in his doctoral thesis of 1945 that the slaves' central desire expressed in song was a return to Africa.[30] Benjamin Mays, in his theological analysis, stressed the otherworldly and compensatory aspect of the Spirituals' meaning.[31] Howard Thurman, the best-known Black mystic, places heavy emphasis on the ontological impulse of the antebellum slaves. For Thurman, the overriding religious meaning of the Spirituals was the slaves' quest for *and* insistence on the affirmation of their *being* that was perpetually being denied by the slave system itself.[32] James Cone leans heavily toward the posture of Lovell who makes an exhaustive case for the sociality inherent in their meaning.[33] Lovell establishes that the religion of the New World African was directly and intimately related to the desire for social and political freedom.[34] The latter stance seems altogether reasonable when one considers the roots out of which the Spiritual form was born—the holistic theological systems of West African traditional religion. The influence of the African form and function on the Spirituals produced a musical literature that was and is a reservoir of the history or social statement that the singers made of the circumstances that impinged upon their lives and that they recorded in African style, in *their music!* Du Bois agrees, underlining the Spirituals as a vehicle of cultural history that demonstrated linkage to Mother Africa.[35]

There seems to be no useful purpose to attempt to establish the theme of the Spirituals' content and purpose but, rather, to note the dominant *themes* that found frequent and identifiable expression, early or late, in the development of this music. The variations of emphasis in interpretation only underscore the umbrella use mentioned above. Cone speaks directly to this point of view: "My contention is that there is a complex world of *thought* underlying the slave songs that has so far escaped analysis. Further theological analysis is needed to uncover this thought and the fundamental world view that it implies."[36]

From a religious point of view, Thurman's list of themes represents a sampling, though not an exhaustive one: God's providence; miraculous deliverance; Jesus, the intimate friend; the crucifixion and resurrection; perseverance; eschatology; existential hope for a better day; personal spiritual need; freedom (in the political sense) and release in death.[37] Lovell's grouping is similar but is based on his conclusions in reference to the social and historical perspectives he sets forth. A partial listing of these "attitudes," as he terms them, follows: Jesus (the love and power of Jesus and the slave's intimate friendship with him), Satan (a conjurer, a trickster, a snake in the grass), Death and Life, Love and Hate (implicit use primarily), Heaven and Hell (firmly believed in the reality of both), War and Peace (the war of slavery and the peace of freedom), Patience and Transitoriness.[38]

Mary Ann Grissom, in her collection of Spirituals, groups the songs thematically as follows: *Death, Heaven and Resurrection, Bible Stories, Exhortation, Service and Personal Experience, Shouting Songs,* and *Songs of Triumph.*[39]

The listings above demonstrate the unique religious insights of the slaves and their sensitivity to their surroundings within the context of the oppressive nature of the slave system and the religious hypocrisy practiced by the slave owners. There is no gainsaying that the oral literature of the Spiritual music was (is) a full and broad, social and theological statement about the difficult world in which the slave community lived.

What are the distinctive features of the Spiritual form? Is it easily recognizable? Are there variables? The answers to the second and third preceding questions are "Yes" within the context of basic characteristics. It is not the intent of this writer to embark on any technical analysis of the musical form and configuration of the Spirituals. There is sufficient material of this kind that is easily available. The work of Henry Krehbiehl is still relevant and accurate, as are the detailed studies of John and Alan Lomax and the more recent work of Hildred Roach already mentioned. The matters of modal characteristics, major versus minor, pentatonic versus diatonic, flatted sevenths, raised sixths, minors without sixths, etc., are beyond the scope of this work. The focus of this inquiry is primarily for a lay audience, and the discussion of technical characteristics is limited to that degree and thus more useful to the general reader.

There is hardly any dispute that rhythm is the key characteristic of African folk music. Rhythm is the key characteristic of Black American music, sacred as well as secular. It follows naturally, then, that the primary characteristic of the Spiritual is rhythm. In similar manner it is helpful to reinforce the contention of African influence, if a general comparison is made between the basic characteristics of African music and the basic characteristics of the faith songs of the slaves. Figure 5 illustrates the similarity mentioned.

In 1963, *Negro Digest* published an essay by this writer entitled "The Soulful Journey of the Negro Spiritual."[40] As a part of demonstrating the direct transference of the Spiritual form to the then developing "freedom song," a brief exposition was made of the basic characteristics of the Negro Spiritual. That listing, with one or two additions, remains instructive in recognizing the fundamental traits of the Spiritual form. The basic characteristics follow with a brief comment and example.

Deep Biblicism. A great number of the Spiritual texts are drawn directly from the Bible with considerable dominance in Old Testament imagery. It is not uncommon to find Old Testament and New Testament references within a single song. Where there is no direct Bible reference that is identifiable, the substance of the truth extolled in a Spiritual is at least biblical in implication. An examination of the body of Afro-American Spirituals will quickly disclose that the primary source of its lyric material is the Holy Bible.

In many instances, a precise textual identification can be made as the direct source of a given Spiritual. The example that follows is of course one of the more familiar instances of Jesus' healing of the blind

FIGURE 5
COMPARISON CHART

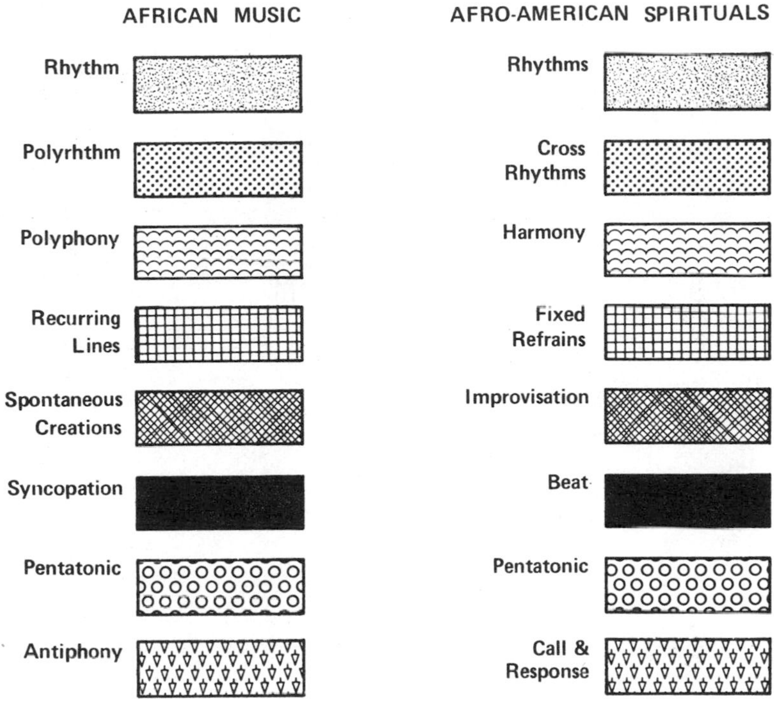

AFRICAN MUSIC		AFRO-AMERICAN SPIRITUALS	
Rhythm		Rhythms	
Polyrhthm		Cross Rhythms	
Polyphony		Harmony	
Recurring Lines		Fixed Refrains	
Spontaneous Creations		Improvisation	
Syncopation		Beat	
Pentatonic		Pentatonic	
Antiphony		Call & Response	

man outside of Jericho. (See Mark 10:46-52 or Luke 18:35-43).

> O, de blin' man stood on de road an' cried.
> O, de blin' man stood on de road an' cried.
> Cryin' O, my Lord, save-a me,
> De blin' man stood on de road an' cried.[41]

Other Spirituals that can be similarly biblically identified are "Dere's a Han' Writin' on de Wall," "John Saw the Holy Number," "Joshua Fit de Battle ob Jericho," and "'Zekiel Saw de Wheel."

Eternality of Message. One of the aspects of the Spirituals' profundity is that many of them carry a timeless message that fits the human circumstance of today. Of course, this is not altogether surprising since the entire body of the music is Bible-based. The message speaks not only to the Black condition out of which it was born but also speaks to the human condition at many points, giving a quality of universality.

One such Spiritual appears below. It speaks of death. Young people may die; the old must die. Kings and peasants alike must face the solitariness of that relentless and implacable fact. The poetry of this Spiritual speaks of that absolutely nondiscriminating event of life—death!

> Oh you got tuh walk-a that lonesome valley,
> You got tuh go tha by yo'sef.
> No one heah to go tha with you,
> You got to go tha by yo'sef.[42]

Another Spiritual of similar universality (within a moral or religious context) is "My Lord's Writin' All de Time."

Rhythmic. The order in which these characteristics are listed is purely arbitrary. If an order were to be established in terms of importance, the rhythm aspect would be a strong contender for the first spot. As rhythm is the fundamental characteristic of African music, so is rhythm the fundamental characteristic of the Afro-American Spiritual. The rhythm(s) varies across the broad range of Spiritual types. Some are slow and plaintive; others are driving and pulsating; still others possess a beat of jubilation.

Whatever the variation, the beat is always there!

The example that illustrates this characteristic is a Spiritual of long tradition in the Black religious experience.

> There's a bright side somewhere,
> There's a bright side somewhere,
> Don't you rest until you find it,*
> There's a bright side *some where.*

(*This line may appear as: "Keep on working for the Master. . . ." The stanzas vary from place to place and church to church depending upon the geographical roots of the members.)

Other spirited numbers of this type would include "Didn't My Lord Deliver Daniel?" "Sinner, Please Don't Let Dis Harvest Pass," and "I'm A-Rollin'."

Given to Improvisation. A brief example will illustrate this quality.

> Don' let nobody turn you aroun',
> Turn you roun', turn you roun'.
> Don' let nobody turn you roun'
> Walking up the King's Highway.

Other verses that could follow in successive repetition might be:

> Don' let ole Satan, etc.
> Don' let temptation, etc.
> Don' let no sinners, etc.

During the confrontation in Birmingham in 1963, the movement interspersed such verses as "Don' let segregation, etc.," Don' let Bull Connor, etc.," and "Don' let no jailhouse, etc.," which reflected in modern times how easily the Spiritual form lent itself to this kind of spontaneous and situational creation of lyrics.

Antiphonal, or Call and Response. If rhythm is the primary characteristic of the Spiritual, in second or third place would be the responsorial mode found in many, many Spirituals. This quality is another strong evidence of an African survival in the New World. African music is rife with this device that finds such effective use in group or communal singing. It should be remembered that the authentic Spiritual form is not given to solo performance; there is frequently a solo or lead line that establishes the melody or a lead line that develops the framework for a choral response from the group. The body of Spiritual literature contains some Spirituals that are more pronounced with this quality than others. "I Heard de Preachin' of de Word o' God" is illustrative of this pronounced responsorial quality.

Lead:	I heard de preachin' of de Elder,
Chorus:	Preachin' de word, preachin' de word,
Lead:	I heard de preachin' of de Elder,
Chorus:	Preachin' de word o' God.
Lead:	How long did it rain? Can any one tell?
Chorus:	Preachin' de word o' God,
Lead:	For forty days an' nights it fell,
Chorus:	Preachin' de word o' God.
Lead:	How long was Jonah in de belly of de whale?
Chorus:	Preachin' de word o' God,
Lead:	'Twas three whole days an' nights he sailed,
Chorus:	Preachin' de word o' God.
Lead:	When I was a mourner I mourned 'til I got through,
Chorus:	Preachin' de word o' God.
Lead:	My knees got acquainted wid de hillside too,
Chorus:	Preachin' de word o' God.
Lead:	I heard de preachin' of de Elder,
Chorus:	Preachin' de word, preachin' de word;
Lead:	I heard de preachin' of de Elder,
Chorus:	Preachin' de word o' God.
All:	Yes, preachin' de word o' God.[43]

Other Spirituals of this kind that possess the pronounced responsorial mode would be those like "In Dat Great Gittin' Up Mornin'," "Oh, My Good Lord, Show Me the Way," and "Swing Low, Sweet Chariot."

Double, or Coded, Meaning. Lovell, in a terse comment cited later in this study (see pp. 67ff.), underscored another Africanism identifiable in the Afro-American Spiritual. There is no way to understand fully the Spiritual without taking into account the device of mask and symbol, or the double meaning. Specific reference will be made as to the different manner in which this use of Spirituals served the slave community.

The classic illustration of a Spiritual that possessed a double meaning is, of course, "Go Down, Moses." Perceptive and intuitive spiritual insights of the New World Africans saw instantly the parallel between their circumstance in this alien land and that of the house of Israel in the land of Egypt. This Spiritual hymn with its majestic cadences was the expressed hope and desire that God would send a "Moses" into the Egypt land of slavery and command the Pharaohs of the slavocracy to "let [his] people go."

The words of this noble hymn, which has universal appeal to all oppressed people, appear following:

> Go down, Moses,
> 'Way down in Egypt land,
> Tell ole Pharaoh,
> To let my people go.
>
> When Israel was in Egypt's land:
> Let my people go,
> Oppressed so hard they could not stand,
> Let my people go.
>
> "Thus spoke the Lord," bold Moses said;
> Let my people go,
> If not I'll smite your first born dead,
> Let my people go.
>
> Go down, Moses,
> 'Way down in Egypt land,
> Tell ole Pharaoh,
> To let my people go.[44]

The family of Spirituals with code meanings includes "Steal Away," "Michael, Row the Boat A-shore," "Walk Together, Children," and "O Mary, Don't You Weep, Don't You Mourn."

Repetitive. The technical phrase to describe this recurring quality of the spiritual song is "incremental iteration." It simply means a pattern or patterns exist in melodic line which repeat with only slight variation. This is frequently reinforced with repetition of the lyric line or verse, providing a double quality of being repetitive. Though obvious, it must be said that both melodic and lyric repetition enhanced the life expectancy of this folk music with this built-in memory facility. One example will suffice here since all of the other examples given reflect to one degree or another, the characteristic quality of being repetitive.

> Were you there, when they crucified my Lord?
> Were you there, when they crucified my Lord?

> Oh, Sometimes, it causes me to tremble, tremble, tremble,
> Were you there, when they crucified my Lord?[45]

Unique Imagery. There is nothing quite like the folk idiom of the antebellum slave. Often tinged with humor or satire, still the pointedness of their message is always perfectly clear. It will suffice for this characteristic merely to cite the titles of several Spirituals to illustrate the fertile imagination of the antebellum Negro. Some of the images they draw are priceless. What can match the word picture of "Sometimes I Feel Like a Motherless Child"[46] or the picturesque "Somebody's Knocking at Your Door"?[47] There is none quite so earthy and yet so faith-filled as "Keep A-Inchin' Along."[48]

Most of the foregoing characteristics are apparent in all genuine Spirituals.

In an extended discussion of the characteristics of the Negro Spiritual an exposition might be given on each of the characteristics listed above. That does not seem necessary for the purposes of this inquiry, though some comments must be made concerning the "coded-meaning" aspect.

The Spirituals that can be identified as "code songs" with historic or legendary connections to slave rebellions reflect still another element of African influence. John Lovell in his discussion of the African influences that are identifiable in the Afro-American Spiritual delineates the use of mask and symbol in African music. Lovell notes that Nketia stresses the wide use of mask and irony among Africans in every type of societal relationship, including songs of insult, history, proverbial songs, and humorous references with two meanings. Thus, double meaning, as a device, is as natural to the Spiritual as ducks to water. Lovell is strong in his conclusion about the presence of this device in the makeup of the Spiritual. "If the interpreter of the spiritual that grew up in America overlooks the mask and symbol, he is displaying remarkable ignorance and indulging in inexcusable inaccuracy."[49]

It takes little deduction, then, to recognize the possibility, probability, and predictability that many Spirituals possess hidden meanings. Harold Courlander uses the term "double-meaning song." Many Spirituals were developed as a part of the slave language to conceal their business from the overseers and the plantation owners. Specifically, hints, signals, and messages encouched in religious jargon of the slaves were often used to point the way or route to freedom and the North. "Steal Away" which has already been mentioned, was reputedly the signal song of Nat Turner's insurrection.

Both Harold Courlander and Hildred Roach acknowledge the use of the double *entendre* in the music of the slaves. They are both clear to say that the double meaning did not always have to do with escape from slavery, though often it did. Roach concedes that the Spirituals were "laden with obsessions about 'freedom land,'" though there is some ambiguity as to whether "Jesus" was intended to be "the God of Christianity, Ntoa, the supernatural spirits of ancestors, or to a Harriet Tubman of the Underground Railroad. Canaan may have depicted a Heaven, a better life to the north, or freedom after Emancipation."[50] Courlander is far more equivocal but does say clearly that "it is a safe assumption that all Negro religious songs were understood by the slaves in the light of their own immediate condition of servitude."[51] This fact stamps clearly upon the musical literature a pointed political significance. Courlander does not agree. He concludes that the Spirituals of the antebellum slave are only religious songs. It must be noted that at this point he is in sharp disagreement with other specialists in the field. James Cone's book *The Spirituals and the Blues: An Interpretation* sets forth the idea that the Spirituals are "the essence of black religion, that is, the experience of trying to be free in the midst of a 'powerful lot of tribulation.'"[52]

The Spirituals that follow might easily have served as religious songs with political significance.

Joshua Fit de Battle of Jerico

Refrain   Joshua fit de battle of Jerico,
Jerico, Jerico,
Joshua fit de battle of Jerico,
An' de walls come tumblin' down.

Stanzas   You may talk about yo' king ob Gideon;
You may talk about yo' man ob Saul;
Dere's none like good ole Joshua
At de battle of Jerico.

Up to de walls ob Jerico
He marched with spear in han'.
"Go blow dem ram horns," Joshua cried,
"Kase de battle am in my han'."

Den de lam ram sheep horns begin to blow;
Trumpets begin to sound.
Joshua commanded de chillen to shout,
An' de walls come tumblin' down.

Steal Away

Refrain   Steal away, steal away,
Steal away to Jesus!
Steal away, steal away home,
I ain't got long to stay here.

Stanza   My Lord calls me,
He calls me by the thunder;
The trumpet sounds within my soul,
I ain't got long to stay here.

Git on Board, Little Chillen

Refrain   Git on board, little chillen,
Git on board, little chillen,
Git on board, little chillen,
Dere's room for many a mo'.

Stanza   De gospel train's a-comin',
I hear it jus' at han';
I hear de car wheels movin'
An' rumblin' thro de lan'.

Didn't My Lord Deliver Daniel?

Refrain   Didn't my Lord deliver Daniel,
Deliver Daniel, deliver Daniel,
Didn't my Lord deliver Daniel,
An' why not every man?

Stanza   He delivered Daniel f'om de lions' den,
Jonah f'om de belly of de whale,
An' de Hebrew children f'om de fiery furnace,
An' why not every man?

Deep River

Refrain   Deep River,
My home is over Jordan,
Deep River, Lord,
I want to cross over into campground.

Stanza   Oh, don't you want to go
To that gospel feast,
That promised land
Where all is peace?

O Mary, Don't You Weep, Don't You Mourn

Refrain   O Mary, don't you weep, don't you mourn,
O Mary, don't you weep, don't you mourn,
Pharaoh's army got drownded,
O Mary, don't you weep.

Stanza   Some of these mornings bright and fair,
Take my wings and cleave the air,
Pharaoh's army got drownded,
O Mary, don't you weep.

Roll, Jordan, Roll

Refrain   Roll, Jordan, roll.
Roll, Jordan, roll,
I want to go heav'n when I die
To hear Jordan roll.

Stanza   O brothers, you ought to have been there;
Yes, my Lord, A-sittin' in the kingdom
To hear Jordan roll.

The development of the Spiritual did not end with the act of emancipation. As mentioned earlier, the Fisk Jubilee Singers helped to make permanent the Spiritual as an American musical art form. However, the manner in which the Fisk singers presented the antebellum songs of faith was a far cry from their original rendering in the praise house and the cotton fields of the South. The domestic and international tour audiences were treated to what can be called a "concertized" form of the Spirituals in order that ears trained to the discipline of European music would not find the inherent repetitive quality boring. The huge success of the Fisk Jubilee Singers is now legendary. A great debt is owed to them and other Black university choirs of that era who kept alive the original Black sacred music of the painful past.

The widespread use of the Spirituals, augmented by the writings of many collectors of folklore, gave rise to still another development in the performance style of Spirituals. R. Nathaniel Dett, in 1914, gave the world of music the first "anthemized" Spiritual, "Listen to the Lambs."[53] Dett, an accomplished musician-composer, used the anthem form and quality, while retaining the Spiritual flavor. He was the pioneer in creating the spiritual-based anthems and inspired many other composers to employ the field Spirituals of an earlier day to provide music in the classical mode. Whalum notes a further development in this regard.

> In 1916 Harry T. Burleigh made a similar contribution when he published a spiritual for solo voice, artistically arranged. Later, many composers followed their lead. James Weldon and J. Rosamond Johnson produced a collection in two different books of spirituals for the solo voice. Hall Johnson began and fully developed his choir, which sang his arrangements primarily.[54]

Before the turn of the century it was Burleigh's influence as a student that had influenced the Czech classicist Anton Dvorak to produce several symphonies based on themes utilizing the idioms of Negro Spirituals.[55]

Many other composers and arrangers followed in this tradition, some of them veritable giants: John W. Work, Sr., Willis Laurence James, William L. Dawson, Clarence Cameron White, Edward Boatner, Frederick Hall, and the tireless Eva Jessy. Among the more recent composers whose influence has been felt in the family of

Spirituals is Undine Smith Moore, a former teacher at Virginia State College.[56]

The wide range of the Spirituals' influence and development has been amazing. It is no wonder, then, that at the height of the demonstrations for social justice and human dignity, that the Black freedom fighters would turn to this mine of music to "create" the freedom songs of the nonviolent movement in the South. More recently, the Alvin Ailey Dance Group has made ingenious use of Spiritual-based themes to create an entire dance repertoire that is entitled "Revelations." Whalum's comment is apt: "The spiritual. . . is the root and trunk of Black music. Its influences are felt today in much that we hear."[57]

The concluding section of this chapter contains a cross section of Spirituals with their musical notations. Several of them have been referred to in the text. Most of the examples are of the field-Spiritual variety in origin if not in form. This type might be heard in any preservice devotional or prayer meeting setting.

Hush! Somebody's Calling My Name

COPYRIGHT, 1923, RENEWAL, 1951
THE RODEHEAVER CO., OWNER
INTERNATIONAL COPYRIGHT SECURED

Arr. by J. B. Herbert.

Roll, Jordan, Roll

COPYRIGHT, 1923, RENEWAL, 1951
THE RODEHEAVER CO., OWNER
INTERNATIONAL COPYRIGHT SECURED

Arr. by J. B. Herbert.

CHORUS.

Roll, Jor-dan, roll,.... Roll, Jor-dan, roll, I want to go to

heav'n when I die To hear Jor-dan roll....

1. O brothers, you ought to have
2. O preachers, you ought to have
3. O sin-ners, you ought to have
4. O mourners, you ought to have

been there; Yes, my Lord, A-sit-tin' in the king-dom

CHORUS.

To hear Jor-dan roll. Roll, Jor-don, roll,.... Roll, Jor-dan, roll, I

want to go to heav'n when I die To hear Jor-dan roll......

The Angels in Heaven Have Changed my Name

COPYRIGHT, 1923. RENEWAL 1951
THE RODEHEAVER CO., OWNER
INTERNATIONAL COPYRIGHT SECURED

Arr. by J. B. Herbert.

I know I've been changed, (O yes,) I know I've been changed, (O yes,)

I know I've been changed, (O yes,) The an-gels in heav'n have

FINE. SOLO.

changed my name. 1. I told the Lord if He'd take my heart,—
2. 'Way down a-bout the Jor-dan stream,—
3. It makes me hap-py when I sing,—

CHORUS.　　　　SOLO.

The an-gels in heav'n have changed my name,—I would-n't de-sert
The an-gels in heav'n have changed my name,—I heard a cry,
The an-gels in heav'n have changed my name,—To know that I

CHORUS.　　　　D. C.

when the bat-tle got hot; The an-gels in heav'n have changed my name.
"I have been re-deemed;" The an-gels in heav'n have changed my name.
have been born a-gain; The an-gels in heav'n have changed my name.

Go Down, Moses

1. When Is-rael was in E-gypt's land: Let my peo-ple go; Op-
2. Thus saith the Lord, bold Mo-ses said, Let my peo-ple go; If

pressed so hard they could not stand, Let my peo-ple go. Go down, Mo-ses,
not, I'll smite your first-born dead, Let my peo-ple go. Go down, Mo-ses,

'Way down in E-gypt land, Tell ole Pha-raoh, Let my peo-ple go.

3 No more shall they in bondage toil,
Let them come out with Egypt's spoil.

4 When Israel out of Egypt came,
And left the proud oppressive land.

5 O, 'twas a dark and dismal night,
When Moses led the Israelites.

6 'Twas good old Moses and Aaron, too,
'Twas they that led the armies through.

7 The Lord told Moses what to do,
To lead the children of Israel through.

8 O come along Moses, you'll not get lost,
Stretch out your rod and come across.

9 As Israel stood by the water side,
At the command of God it did divide.

10 When they had reached the other shore,
They sang the song of triumph o'er.

11 Pharaoh said he would go across,
But Pharaob and his host were lost.

12 O Moses the cloud shall clear the way,
A fire by night, a shade by day.

13 You'll not get lost in the wilderness,
With a lighted candle in your breast.

14 Jordan shall stand up like a wall,
And the walls of Jericho shall fall.

15 Your foes shall not before you stand,
And you'll posess fair Canaan's land

16 'Twas just about in harvest-time,
When Joshua led his host divine.

17 O let us all from bondage flee,
And let us all in Christ be free.

18 We need not always weep and moan.
And wear these slavery chains forlorn.

Steal Away

May be sung by one voice, or in unison.

Steal a - way, steal a - way, Steal a - way to Je - sus!

Steal a - way, steal a - way home, I aint got long to stay here.

1. My Lord calls me, He calls me by the thun - der; The
2. Green trees are bend - ing, Poor sin - ner stan's a - tremb-ling; The
3. Tomb-stones are burst-ing, Poor sin - ner stan's a - tremb-ling; The
4. My Lord calls me, He calls me by the light - ning; The

trump-et sounds with - in my soul, I ain't got long to stay here.

It's Me.

Dr. A. M. Townsend.

Plaintive, not too fast.

It's me, it's me, O Lord, Stand-ing in the need of prayer;

FINE.

It's me, it's me, O Lord, Stand-ing in the need of prayer.

It's me,

1. Not my brother, but it's me, O Lord, Stand-ing in the need of prayer;
2. Not my sis-ter, but it's me, O Lord, Stand-ing in the need of prayer;
3. Not my mother, but it's me, O Lord, Stand-ing in the need of prayer;
4. Not my eld-er, but it's me, O Lord, Stand-ing in the need of prayer;

D. C.

Not my brother, but it's me, O Lord, Stand-ing in the need of prayer.
Not my sis-ter, but it's me, O Lord, Stand-ing in the need of prayer.
Not my mother, but it's me, O Lord, Stand-ing in the need of prayer.
Not my eld-er, but it's me, O Lord, Stand-ing in the need of prayer.

Walk With Me.

E. C. Deas.

CHORUS. *Moderato.*

I want Je-sus to walk with me, (walk with me,) I want Je-sus to walk with me; (with me;) All a-long my pil-grim jour-ney, I want Je-sus to walk with me.

VERSES.

1. In my tri-als, walk with me, walk with me, In my tri-als, walk with me, walk with me, When the shades of life are fall-ing, Lord, I want Je-sus to walk with me.
2. In my sor-rows, walk with me, walk with me, In my sor-rows, walk with me, walk with me, When my heart with-in is ach-ing, Lord, I want Je-sus to walk with me.
3. In my troub-les, walk with me, Lord, walk with me, In my troub-les, walk with me, walk with me, When my life be-comes a bur-den, Lord, I want Je-sus to walk with me.

Somebody's Knocking At Your Door.

Work Brothers.

CHORUS. *Moderato.*

Some-bod-y's knock-ing at your door, Some-bod-y's knock-ing at your door;

O sin - ner, why don't you answer? Somebody's knocking at your door.

FINE.

D. S.—*O sin-ner, why don't you answer? Somebody's knocking at your door.*

1. Knock like Je - sus, Some-bod - y's knock-ing at your door;
2. Can't you hear Him? Some-bod - y's knock-ing at your door;
3. An - swer Je - sus, Some-bod - y's knock-ing at your door;
4. Je - sus calls you, Some-bod - y's knock-ing at your door;
5. Can't you trust Him? Some-bod - y's knock-ing at your door;

D. S.

Knocks like Je - sus, Some-bod - y's knock-ing at your door.
Can't you hear Him? Some-bod - y's knock-ing at your door.
An - swer Je - sus, Some-bod - y's knock-ing at your door.
Je - sus calls you, Some-bod - y's knock-ing at your door.
Can't you trust Him? Some-bod - y's knock-ing at your door.

"I Love the Lord, 5
He Heard My Cry"

Black Meter Music

Slavery in the New World that began with those "twenty negars" from that Dutch man-of-war swiftly became, by the beginning of the eighteenth century, the most despicable form of human bondage in modern history. Its legal end came with the executive order of Abraham Lincoln, conventionally called by some "The Emancipation Proclamation." The president's signature in 1863 hammered the final nail into the coffin of chattel slavery in America. By the end of the decade, most of the apparatus of the slave system had disappeared. Four million slaves were *free!*

The transition from slavery to freedom for the New World African was of monumental social and personal significance. It is clearly reflected in the new life-style of the people, the quickened pace of personal and group development, and the more broadly established "visible church" as the primary institution of Black life in America. This development, a social statement in itself, was the sure evidence of the expansion of the religious faith and practice of Black people.

What is this meter music to which we have turned our attention? In the life of early colonial America the singing of psalms (of the Bible) was an integral part of worship and religious instruction. The practice of psalm singing was widespread, especially among those religious groups who expressed concern about "the religious instruction of slaves." In 1707, Dr. Watts, a minister and physician, published *Hymns and Spiritual Songs,* a collection of religious poems that was warmly received throughout the colonies.

It could be argued, on the basis of the history of the meter music

FIGURE 6

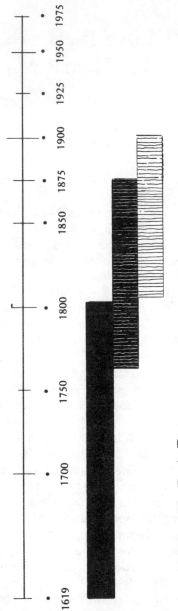

TIME BAR

Black Sacred Music

Period of Development & Dominance

 SLAVES UTTERANCES/Moans, Chants, Cries for Deliverance

SPIRITUALS/Faith-Songs, Sorrow Songs, Plantation Hymns, etc.

METER MUSIC/Watts, Wesley, Sankey et al.

phenomenon in North America, that the time period for this style of religious singing should be set much earlier than the Time Bar indicates. However, it must be remembered that for Black people to have stamped their identity on the meter music of Dr. Watts and others, this stamping would sequentially follow the establishing of a music tradition of their own making, the Afro-American religious folk song, or Spiritual.

Some clear distinction must be made between the normal American phenomenon of meter music and the Black use of Dr. Watts's hymns. The distinction is necessary in order to grasp a clear historical perspective of the period under consideration. The singing of psalms and, shortly thereafter, the singing of metered music were in current practice in the early eighteenth century. Such singing came into its heyday during the Great Awakening under Jonathan Edwards and remained popular through the Second Awakening. Singing psalms and metered music became one of the hallmarks of the camp meetings that were so much a part of frontier-style religion. In many respects this kind of singing was the precursor of "white Spirituals" which some writers, in error, believe to be the source of the Afro-American Spiritual. *This is not the meter music of our concern!*

The meter music of which we speak is that music identical in lyrics to Dr. Watts and others of similar genre but appropriated by Blacks for their own specific religious and worship needs: "When Christianity seized the Black experience the worshippers took hold of whatever was shared with them and made it into a music of their own. This was not plagiarism. It was an honest effort to give God their best."[1]

This meter music demonstrated clear evidences of the input of the oral tradition which has been mentioned so frequently.

The historical period embraced by the development and dominance of Black meter music is an overlapping era of both slavery and freedom. The meter style of singing, like the historical period, was a transitional form that bridged the slavery and Reconstruction periods and persisted in evidence until the beginning of the twentieth century. The Great Awakening, with its fervor, demanded livelier music, and the Watts-style hymns with their freshness and vitality filled the bill. The bright imagery of Dr. Watts and the Wesley brothers in these hymn poems found new friends in the antebellum slave community.

As far as can be determined, the broad use of these hymn texts in sacred services reached its ascendancy around 1875. Wendel Whalum specifically assigns the design and modal form of this "meter singing" to Black Baptists.[2] As the structured congregations of the Black community increased by leaps and bounds hard on the heels of Emancipation, so did the frequency of the use of these hymn texts increase. Whalum has an incisive comment concerning this period:

> The Black Methodists and Baptists endorsed Watts' hymns, but the Baptists "blackened" them. They virtually threw out the meter signature and rhythm and before 1875 had begun a new system which, though based on the style of singing coming from England to America in the eighteenth century, was drastically different from it. It was congregational singing much like the spiritual had been in which the text was retained.[3]

Whalum has already intimated above that there is a direct relationship to the Spiritual. The presence of a distinct "beat" and obvious free syncopation makes apparent the direct relationship. Add to that the performance which always has the responsorial mode—the call and response device—where a leader recites the line in singsong fashion, followed by the congregation in unison singing of the text.

The Watts-style hymn text, as we shall refer to this body of Black sacred music, generally followed the quatrain formula (four lines). Occasionally, two additional lines appeared, often repetitive of lines that already appeared. This produced a six-line stanza. The six-line form is the exception rather than the rule.

The meter music was (is) usually performed without accompaniment of instruments. The style of performance was born in slavery when there were no organs or pianos and reached its peak during that period of church development when organs and pianos did not have a priority on the institution's agenda. In fact, in all of this writer's experience, no *authentic* meter music with accompaniment has been heard. It would appear that it cannot be accompanied and properly rendered. The blended voices of a congregation and the communal rhythm idiom become at once the rendered hymn *and* the accompaniment.

Whatever the Euro-American words, the developing Black

religious community not only gave the Watts-style hymn their unique musical imprint, but also in their hearts they were singing to the same God of the Spirituals who was vastly different from the God of the slave owners and overseers. The God of the Spirituals had delivered them from the bondage of "Egypt"; the new hymns were fashioned to suit the use of the newly freed former slaves. Their previous experience with God had been salutary—they had been freed! In the bewilderment of the postwar milieu, that same God, now extolled in the meter music borrowed along the road to freedom, would serve them in the present as he had in the past. The optimism and confidence encouched in the Watts hymns, along with those appropriated from the *Bay Psalm Book* or the *Wesleyan Hymnal,* strengthened them to face the challenge of Reconstruction and the disappointment of post-Reconstruction. One such familiar common meter hymn describes that spirit:

> I love the Lord: he heard my cries,
> And pitied every groan:
> Long as I live, when troubles rise,
> I'll hasten to his throne.

> I love the Lord: he bowed his ear,
> And chased my grief away:
> Oh, let my heart no more despair
> While I have breath to pray.

> The Lord beheld me sore distressed;
> He bade my pains remove;
> Return, my soul, to God, thy rest,
> For thou hast known his love.[4]

The meter hymn in no way displaced the Spiritual music. It simply represented an expanding religious consciousness and changed social context that was reflected in the growing musical repertoire of the ex-slaves. There are numerous examples that illustrate that the meter music served (lyrically) to feed already "established" Spirituals through the process of "coupling"—that is, integrating the Euro-American lyrics into a familiar Spiritual number:

> Spiritual Refrain:
> He didn't have to wake me, but He did.
> He didn't have to wake me, but He did.

> Woke me up this morning, and started
>   me on my way.
> He didn't have to wake me, but He did.
> Verse: (from a hymn)
> Amazin' Grace, How sweet the sound,
> That saved a wretch like me,
> I once was lost, but now I'm found,
> Was blind but now I see.[5]

It must be conceded that the original religious folk music faded into the background somewhat. Since freedom had come, some sentiment developed early on that this music hammered out in the slave communities of the South was no longer of the moment.

> . . . these songs passed through a period when the front ranks of the Negro race would have been willing to let them die. Immediately following Emancipation those ranks revolted against everything connected with slavery, and among those things were the Spirituals. It became a sign of not being progressive or educated to sing them. This was a natural reaction, but, nevertheless, a sadly foolish one. It was left for the older generation to keep them alive by singing them at prayer meetings, . . . experience meetings and revivals. . . .[6]

The formation of the Fisk Jubilee Singers and the Black college choirs and choruses who became their heirs preserved in permanent form the baseline musical art form upon which all American music stands.

The Period of Meter Music

As the Time Bar indicates, the Black use of Watts-style hymns began around 1807–1810. (See Figure 6.) This does not mean to suggest, as pointed out earlier, that the Watts-type hymn poems had just arrived on the American scene. This is the identifiable date when these hymn poems began to have some usage among Black people, principally those in the antebellum slave community. The use of the lyrics, in one way or another, in Black religious song steadily increased, showing a marked growth that paralleled the incidence of literacy among Blacks, slave or free. There had to be some relationship between the breadth of literacy and the interest in these "new" hymns. The oral tradition served the religious folk songs of the Negro in straight-line fashion. The meter music was developed in the oral tradition though it did not originate in that tradition. The origin of the lyrics, of course, was Euro-American in character. Thus, the general period of development and dominance of Black meter music is 1807–1900.

It is patently obvious that the era of meter music's development and dominance spans three distinct historical periods of Black people's sojourn on these shores: slavery, Reconstruction, and post-Reconstruction. The overlapping developmental periods of the Spiritual and meter music both parallel the period of the slavocracy, and it does not seem profitable to repeat that which has already been discussed under the Afro-American Spiritual. (See chapter 4.)

The Period of Reconstruction—1865–1877

Slavery had been ended and four million ex-slaves were free. The hopes and dreams of departed forebears had been realized. Following Lee's surrender at Appomattox in 1865, in swift succession the Thirteenth, Fourteenth, and Fifteenth Amendments of the Constitution were ratified and signed into law by Congress. Slavery was abolished, ex-slaves were citizens, and they were guaranteed the right of the ballot. Sizable numbers of the newly freed Blacks moved North and to the frontiers of the West, but the largest number of them remained in the South, resettling either as modest landowners or as sharecroppers. In spite of their poor preparation for the new mobility afforded by the Emancipation Proclamation, significant numbers of ex-slaves began to take seriously the participatory responsibilities of citizenship. During the decade that followed the ending of the War, Blacks were to be found in public and elected offices all across the South, in numbers unequaled until the early seventies of the twentieth century. The Freedmen's Bureau was established by the federal government as an organized attempt to facilitate the adjustment of the Black community from slave status to an allegedly free society.

It was not an easy task. The social and economic changes induced by the freeing of the slaves were immense, but they were further complicated by the advent of the industrial revolution in the North.[7]

Caught up in the middle of this national flux were the four million recently freed Blacks. The years following the end of the Civil War held some high promises. The rumors of "forty acres and a mule" induced visions of broad land ownership and full citizenship in the republic. Such was not to be. The bitterness of the South in defeat and headlong rush for profits in the industrial North resulted in a crossfire of vested interests that Black people feel even today.

In spite of these crosscurrents, during the first decade following the war Blacks did settle hundreds of thousands of acres all across the South. Some ambitious business ventures were begun, most of them destined to fail. Under the aegis of the Freedmen's Bureau, medical services for Blacks, heretofore unheard of, were established and the life expectancy of the Black people measurably extended. Such services were in addition to the Bureau's relief-agency role of reducing suffering among the ex-slaves. John Hope Franklin notes that the most important work of the Bureau was in the field of education.[8] That agency, as an enabler, encouraged and supported the founding of schools for the ex-slaves at every level with classes in literacy training scheduled morning, afternoon, and night. It was during this period that most of the church-related colleges were established.

The independent Black churches became the second most important agency, offering both spiritual and material relief during Reconstruction. Membership and strength among the older Negro denominations (African Methodist Episcopal [A.M.E.] and African Methodist Episcopal Zion [A.M.E.Z.]) quadrupled, and among the new churches (Baptists, Colored Methodist Episcopal [now Christian Methodist Episcopal, C.M.E.]) the growth was phenomenal.

In the political arena, the ex-slaves took seriously the opportunity for political involvement. The legislatures of every Southern state had Negro representation that varied from numerical superiority in South Carolina to token participation in Texas and Virginia.[9] It is generally conceded that the laws across the South enacted in this period were as progressive and forward-looking as any to date. Among the laws passed which were of significant long-range importance was the repeal of laws requiring land ownership as the qualification to the ballot and the establishment of a universally free public educational system.

These positive developments did not come about easily. The ex-slaves met a continuing hostility from the defeated white Southerners who resented the loss of their slave property, the fact of a ravaged agrarian economy, and the increasing influence in public affairs of their former chattel. Added to this was the competition, North and South, in the job market. Blacks possessed a wider diversity in occupational skills then than has been the case since. The crass use of cheap Negro labor to thwart unionization and the labor movement's adamant stance of exclusion for Blacks soon closed the door of the skilled labor force to Black artisans.[10] The great influx of European immigrants into the labor force, along with the impact of rapid industrialization in the nation, further narrowed the employment opportunities for the ex-slaves. By default the ex-slaves were soon to be forced back to many of the plantations they had left to work free where they had once worked as slaves. Sharecropping became the legitimate first cousin to slavery. William A. Jones, Jr., lecturing in Rochester, said of this strange twist of history, "Lincoln didn't free the slaves; he fired them!"[11]

Soon the infamous Black Codes were spawned under the specter of "the Black revenge." Rutherford B. Hayes rose to the presidency, and the slide downhill of Black folks' fortunes was begun in earnest. The great hopes of Reconstruction were destroyed by the reality of post-Reconstruction. Figure 7 graphically demonstrates how the flow of history in this period ended in political disaster for the ex-slaves.

The Period of Post-Reconstruction—1877–1897

The swearing in of Rutherford B. Hayes, in retrospect, sounded the death knell of Black folks' hopes for minimal reparation for their enforced enslavement. Despite the campaign promises "to heal the wounds of the nation" and "guarantee the right of the ballot to every citizen, irrespective of race," Hayes's first act of "healing" was to remove the troops from the South, as part of the bargain struck for Tilden's withdrawal.[12] This flagged the posture of his administration as being unconcerned about the physical or political welfare of the ex-slaves. With increasing momentum, state by state, legislature by legislature, the wheels were set in motion to nullify all of the gains made in behalf of Black people during Reconstruction. It was the darkest period of America's political history with the single exception of the Nixon era. The executive, judicial, and legislative branches of government, state and federal, in a step-by-step process stripped from the Negro almost all of the political dignity that had been gained by

FIGURE 7
FLOW OF HISTORY

1. SLAVERY

Chattel slavery obtained from 1619 to 1861. Considered by many historians as worst form of human bondage in Western history.

2. EMANCIPATION

Executive order of Lincoln freed 4.8 million slaves. Passage of 13th, 14th, 15th Amendments followed.

3. RECONSTRUCTION

Freedmen, despite handicaps, began ambitious participation in political process, finding representation at local, state, and federal levels.

4. POST-RECONSTRUCTION

Marked by Rutherford Hayes's ascendancy to presidency and subsequent withdrawal of troops from South. This action flagged compromise on Negro's political equality.

5. PLESSY V. FERGUSON

Following a period when rights and gains of Blacks were nullified by legislative, judicial, and executive branches of government at state and federal levels, segregation imposed with sanction of Supreme Court.

emancipation and during the all too brief period called Reconstruction. So complete was the disfranchisement that this period closed with the infamous *Plessy* v. *Ferguson* Supreme Court decision, affirming with the stamp of federal sanction the separation of the races on the basis of color. A physical slavery had been replaced by psychological slavery.

It was this severe turn of events, gradual at first and later pronounced, with which the ex-slaves had to maintain some sense of personal and collective equilibrium. The unrelenting process of disfranchisement was just one side of the coin. Parallel to what was happening in the courts and the state legislatures was the advent of the terror tactics of embittered Southern demagogues. The latter part of the nineteenth century was punctuated with the activities of groups like the Ku Klux Klan or the Knights of the White Camelia.[13] Lynch mobs were common and the use of physical intimidation, coupled with specious state laws like the grandfather clause, resulted in the total disfranchisement of the ex-slaves.

This was the world of events for Black folks in the period of the greatest use of meter music (1875–1900). An examination of its musical idiom and relationship to the Spiritual which influenced its performance give some clues as to how its development, presence, and use fortified Black folks spiritually.

Social Significance of Black Meter Music

It has been firmly established among anthropologists that one can discern much about a group of people by their music. As Alan Lomax asserts, folk music serves as a "culture indicator."[14] The music of the slaves, in its style and content, has much to say about the people, their circumstance, and how they responded to a specific social context. Or it might manifest a lack of response through some escape mechanism or device that shuts out an unbearable reality.

It follows, then, that the variations of music sung by post-slavery Black people in this republic, whether created, doctored, appropriated, blackened—*whatever*—would also be in some measure an index to their response to the changing and shifting social context. Black meter music, in particular, illustrates this general rule of thumb. It is included under the umbrella of Black folk music because it has been influenced primarily by the Spiritual music art form, though technically it is a bastard form of the music mentioned. Its form and performance, however, persisted by means of the oral tradition which gave birth and life to the Spiritual.

It has been mentioned earlier in this chapter that Black people were familiar with and participated in "meter singing" prior to Emancipation. However, it was *after* the Emancipation Proclamation that meter music came into real ascendancy. Since the lyrics were from the dominant white culture, and slaves were now *free,* the impulse for imitation was natural and understandable, religiously and otherwise. Given the association that the Spirituals had with the slave experience and the quest for expanding the Black people's religious life and expression, the meter music found fertile ground for development and use immediately following the freeing of the slaves. So sharp was the decline in the use of Spirituals in formal worship services that the great body of them might have become extinct had it not been for their popularization through the national and international tours of the Fisk Jubilee Singers that began around 1875. The worldwide acclaim gave a new dimension and credibility to a body of music that for several years was in danger of near total eclipse. Much of what happened, in retrospect, was influenced by the changes in the religious practices and increased mobility of the Black worshiping community.

Prior to the Emancipation Proclamation, the great majority of Black people on the North American continent were *(a)* in the South and *(b)* chattel slaves. (See Figure 1.) It follows, then, that the greatest amount of religious life was in the antebellum slave society. That society was, for the most part, rural. Until 1800, only Charleston, South Carolina, and New Orleans, Louisiana, were considered cities. That demographic fact prescribed a mobility to the slave community which was, at best, limited. The broadest exchange for personal and social development was limited by the size of the plantation to which a slave belonged and the stringency with which the slave code was imposed, e.g., prohibition against travel. At the time of emancipation, the slaves were supposedly free to go, move about, emigrate to the urban communities, flock to the growing towns in the South, learn to read, organize churches, join those already in existence—in other words, they now had an expanded *social mobility!*

The clearest evidence of this mobility was the rapid rise in the organization and growth of "historic" Black churches. There were a few independent Black churches that began in the late eighteenth century, North and South, but no great numbers of physical structures in proportion to the total Black population appeared until after the Emancipation Proclamation. Many of the freedmen flocked to the "established churches": African Methodist Episcopal, African Methodist Episcopal Zion, and the "free" Baptist congregations that antedated Emancipation. The overwhelming majority of freedmen became Baptists, as evidenced by the disproportionate ratio that persists even to the present. Several factors contributed to this denominational imbalance of the past and present. First, the Black people were strongly attracted by the water rite of immersion practiced by Baptists and to the Baptist style of worship "because they could identify points of continuity between their African heritage and Baptist practice."[15] Secondly, it was simpler to organize a Baptist church than any other and the democractic tradition of individual church government lent itself easily to the devices of newly freed ex-slaves. New church houses began to multiply all over the South and North. The Freedmen's Bureau helped to make these church houses new centers of community focus, making them into literacy centers as they took on the gargantuan task of reducing the widespread illiteracy imposed by slavery. Education and religion proceeded among the freedmen hand in hand. Thus, the great religious energy that was forced to satisfy itself with the services of the cane-brake and the brush-arbors was released and directed into transforming the "invisible church" into a thoroughly "visible church." The Black religious experience now turned to building and acquiring physical structures.

As indicated earlier, all of the historic Black denominations grew phenomenally, but none like the Baptists. As early as 1880, Black Baptists in the South had grown strong enough to form the Foreign Mission Convention of the United States of America with 151 delegates present at its initial meeting in Montgomery, Alabama.[16] In 1886, some six hundred delegates assembled in St. Louis, Missouri. Out of this meeting was founded the American National Baptist Convention.[17] A third major Black Baptist Convention came into being in 1893 with its avowed purpose to train leaders with the Black

Church. It was named The Baptist Educational Convention. A year later, at the fourteenth annual meeting of the Foreign Mission Convention, a resolution calling for a merger of these three major Black Baptist bodies into one organization was presented. In 1895, in Atlanta, Georgia, the National Baptist Convention, U.S.A., Inc., was born, with E. C. Morris as its first president.[18]

The Baptist experience was paralleled in proportionate growth among the three major Methodist bodies, the older A.M.E. and A.M.E.Z. and the newly formed C.M.E. The Northern (White) Methodists had a sizable Black following also, but it was in these historic Black churches that the music of the forefathers was preserved and varied as a reflection of the social context in which they grew and developed.

The rapid growth and development of the "visible church" had very much to do with the broad participation of the freedmen in civil and political affairs. The Freedmen's Bureau looked to and received critical help from the hundreds of Black churches that sprang up overnight following the war. The dissemination of information, the formation of schools, the distribution of aid, political instruction— all had a prime focus in Black churches. It was not long before the Black Church was firmly established as the primary institution of influence in the lives of Black people in the North as well as the South. This alone evidenced a certain kind of independence in the Black community that had never been exhibited on so large a scale. To be sure, there were some enterprising free Blacks prior to the Emancipation Proclamation, but the population statistics are very persuasive. For every free Black, there were ten slaves! Thus, before the war, the slaves had no opportunity to exhibit independence of any kind; but after the war, the growth of the institutionalized Black Church demonstrated a distinct surge in the independence of the Black community.

It is to be noted again that the broad range of Negro skills— embodied in artisans of every stripe directed to Black concerns— contributed an element of self-sustenance to the Black community that it had never had before. The skills and crafts had always been used for the objects of "massa's" priority; now these skills were utilized for the priorities of the developing Black community, most of it religiously oriented.

The widespread political activity of the freedmen in some ways affected their outlook on life and religious practice. The period of Reconstruction was so brief and nullification of the gains made so swift that it is difficult to read in religious practice just what the Black man anticipated in this regard. It is inescapable that the betrayal of the Negro politically during that period called post-Reconstruction had its distinct effect. The early vision gloriously produced the Thirteenth, Fourteenth, and Fifteenth Amendments and the political participation prior to 1875. The letdown following the removal of the troops from the South forced Blacks again to rise above the bizarre reality. The choice and use of music very often took on a familiar compensatory character. There is also clear evidence in their choice of lyrics of an unfailing trust in God. In the next section, we shall peruse some of the special favorites of the Black meter music tradition with a view toward catching a reflection of what Black people in Reconstruction and post-Reconstruction were saying to themselves religiously.

Profile of Black Meter Music

The use of "Dr. Watts" hymns for meter singing seems generally to have been dominated by the Baptists (all persuasions). Any discussion of the music itself must begin with the popular reservoir of Black Baptist hymn tradition, *The Baptist Standard Hymnal*. In the publisher's note, it is interesting to read a part of the rationale for compiling such a hymnal under a historic Black denomination's auspices.

> It must be noted that there seems now to be a tendency to get away from that fervency of spirit and song that characterized the church and altar worship of other days, and which contributes so much to the stability of our religion. With the thought, therefore, of the preservation of the good old soul stirring hymns of days gone by, together with many standard selections and favorites and contributions . . . from members of the Hymnal Committee, and a large number of other worthy productions of the present generation, "The Baptist Standard Hymnal" has been compiled.[19]

This section of the discussion of meter music will lean heavily on this source since there is hardly any place else to look. This writer has either read or perused nearly a hundred books that discuss Black music directly or indirectly. Most of these volumes bow naturally to the Spiritual as the root of all indigenous American music. If the discussion is chronological (and it usually is), at the juncture of the act of emancipation no further word is mentioned of *Black sacred music*. Infrequently, some mention is made in passing of gospel and the influence that blues and jazz had upon the gospel idiom. But nowhere in serious discussion has this writer been able to find anything of substance on the Black use of "Dr. Watts" hymns, and others, in meter singing. Eileen Southern's *The Music of Black Americans* (552 pages) makes little mention of "meter singing" though there are three references to "lining a hymn," a chief characteristic of meter music. This is only a specific instance of a larger void. After one leaves the Spiritual, as far as research is concerned there is very little record of the unique brand of sacred music that prevails in large measure in the Black folk churches in America. The fact that the many forms of this music are still intact again buttresses the argument of an "oral tradition" in Black religious music. So much for this digression.

Let us turn now to a technical definition of *meter,* or *metre. The Baptist Standard Hymnal* provides an explanation:

> The term Metre or Meter, is a Greek word and properly belongs to poetry, from whence it is transferred to music. Metre is the Measure, or the Standard by which the long and short syllables in the verses of a hymn are rhythmically and definitely arranged into groups of syllables called poetic "Feet." Each "Foot," having a distinctive name, is to poetry what a measure is, in many respects, to music. Very little is known of the actual way Greek verse was adapted to singing tones, yet it is safe to assume that every long syllable was sung to a longer tone and every short syllable to a shorter tone. Modern verse is set to a larger variety of patterns of long and short tones, provided that the "Accented" Syllables match with "Accented" Tones. The regular recurrence of the "Accent" constitutes and determines the Metre of the line or verse. In a modern Hymnal a very large number of forms may be represented but the form of every hymn-tune depends on the verse-form to which it belongs. Out of four or five types of "Feet," developed the fundamental rhythm of modern music and its types of Metre. Of the many recognized "Feet," Iambic with lines sometimes of 10 or more syllables, Dactylic, Amphibrachic, Anapestic and Trochial are the chief types. . . . The most frequently used Meters are: Common Metre (C. M.), Common Hallelujah Metre (C. H. M.), Long Metre (L. M.), Long Particular Metre (L. P. M.), Hallelujah Metre (H. M.), Short Metre (S. M.), Short Particular Metre (S. P. M.).[20]

It is obvious that neither the antebellum slaves nor the freedmen were privy to the kind of meter singing that is described above. They did hear members of the dominant society singing meter, and the words of meter hymns (Watts especially and to a lesser degree Wesley and later Sankey) had a catchy attraction. Ninety percent of the meter singing that this writer has heard, or *heard of,* has been Common Meter that is still used in the churches of the masses. It is hardly ever sung in Black middle-class churches and seldom ever in the churches of the more highly structured denominations.

Common Meter and occasionally Long Meter and still less frequently Short Meter, as sung by Blacks, had a distinctive flavor. It does not, nor could it ever, fit the regimen of the technical analysis above. The slaves and later the freedmen got the hang of it and then gave it a soul imprint. The end product is the Black meter music tradition. It cannot be described accurately in narrative, and the reader's appreciation of this musical art form will be deepened upon hearing an example of this singing (for example, on a cassette tape that is available through the publishers of this volume).

The Baptist Standard Hymnal is the best source and collection of hymn tunes for hymns that fit the meter mold of this tradition. At the end of this chapter, there is a sample grouping of meter hymns which are typical and taken directly from the hymnal. Only the words appear (as shown), and they have been placed in the hymnbook in just this manner so that the user of the hymnal knows that this is the music to be sung in meter style.

The hymns at the end of this chapter appear without their hymn tunes, but the meter corresponds to the meter tradition, and the hymns are frequently sung in the mold and form of the Black meter music tradition. (The cassette tape mentioned above will illustrate how one poem can be sung to its familiar hymn tune and then performed in the Black meter music tradition.)

The leader of the meter music, deacon, preacher, or song leader, gives two lines to the assembled worshipers in singsong fashion, following which, almost with overlap, the general body of worshipers take up on perfect cue, those same two lines and sing it in "meter." The recitation of another two lines completes the quatrain, and the ensuing stanzas are sung in the same manner until the hymn poem is completed. Often the signal of the end of a meter hymn would be what is described in the West as the "humming" of two lines, but in the Black Baptist tradition it is known as "moaning" or "mourning." In the early days following the Emancipation Proclamation, the singing of meter music was the accepted style of congregational singing, but with the advent of piano and organ it became the sermon hymn just before the preaching of the gospel. The latter practice still remains in many churches of the South, but nowhere is it done quite like it is in the Wheat Street Baptist Church of Atlanta, Georgia, under the ministry of William Holmes Borders.

What was the basis of the attraction of the meter form for the ex-slaves? First of all, the quatrain form, or four-line form, of the Watts-style hymn lent itself to easy rote memory during a period when illiteracy was widespread. Following the war, as literacy increased, the quatrain, like the Bible, was a natural and easily available practice ground for the new skill. Secondly, as physical structures developed, formal worship services, as distinct from the religious meetings of the praise houses held on the plantations, began to supplant the earlier forms of worship associated with the "invisible church." The "new" hymns fitted this "new" arrangement. The day of open-end religious meetings had passed with the end of slavery. Thirdly, and just as important as the other two, an expanding religious consciousness—influenced by the new conditions of the social context—gave to the ex-slaves a sense of a larger religious identity beyond the slave consciousness forced upon them for so long. Now they were *free* and would sing the music of the larger community about them as an assertion that they took seriously their belonging. It must be remembered that in spite of the profound theological concepts found in the Spiritual music, the ex-slaves' faith was not systematized as was the traditional African religion of the Motherland. In its development it did not copy the form and systems of Western Christianity which trickled down to them. They had digested the substance in the order that survival required. The advent of the meter music phenomenon had a stabilizing effect upon their faith which was necessary in the adjustments to the new social context. This stability in religious life played an important role in the institutionalizing of the Black religious experience. The Black meter music tradition, as much as the Spiritual music art form upon which it was founded musically, contributed largely to welding the great mass of newly free ex-slaves into a rather formidable institutional influence by the end of the nineteenth century. In the face of the reverses suffered under post-Reconstruction, that strong institutional influence in the lives of most Black folks was the citadel of hope that kept Job's spiritual heirs "singing the Lord's song in a strange land."

Two examples of the meter music hymn poem appear below for the sake of illustrating the imagery of Dr. Watts and the confidence of the religious sentiment it carried.

The first example expresses the confidence of God's individual concern, which reinforces in the worshiper a sense of meaningful self-worth:

Now Is the Accepted Time
S. M.

1. Now is the accepted time,
   Now is the day of grace;
   Now, sinners, come without delay,
   And seek the Savior's face.

2. Now is the accepted time,
   The Savior calls to-day;
   To-morrow it may be too late—
   Then why should you delay?

3. Now is the accepted time,
   The gospel bids you come;
   And every promise in his word
   Declares there yet is room.

4. Lord, draw reluctant souls,
   And feast them with thy love;
   Then will the angels clap their wings
   And bear the news above.[21]

The next example illustrates the realization that separation from God is intolerable. This is an all-time Watts favorite within the Black tradition:

C. M.

1. That awful day shall surely come,—
   Th' appointed hour makes haste,—
   When I must stand before my Judge,
   And pass the solemn test.

2. Thou lovely Chief of all my joys,
    Thou Sovereign of my heart,
   How could I bear to hear thy voice
    Pronounce the sound, "Depart!"

3. O, wretched state of deep despair,
    To see my God remove,
   And fix my dreadful station where
    I must not taste his love!

4. Jesus, I throw my arms around,
    And hang upon thy breast;
   Without one gracious smile from thee,
    My spirit cannot rest.

5. O, tell me that my worthless name
    Is graven on thy hands;
   Show me some promise in thy book,
    Where my salvation stands.[22]

To illustrate the metered hymn which has its own hymn tune, we turn again to another Isaac Watts favorite:

1. Alas! and did my Savior bleed?
    And did my Sov'reign die?
   Would He devote that sacred head
    For such a worm as I?

2. Was it for crimes that I have done
    He groaned upon the tree?
   Amazing pity! grace unknown!
    And love beyond degree!

3. Well might the sun in darkness hide,
    And shut his glories in,
   When Christ, the mighty Maker, died,
    For man, the creature's sin.

4. Thus might I hide my blushing face,
    While His dear cross appears;
   Dissolve my heart in thankfulness,
    And melt mine eyes to tears.

5. But drops of grief can ne'er repay
    The debt of love I owe:
   Here, Lord, I give myself away,—
    'Tis all that I can do.[23]

This hymn evidences by widespread use the centrality of Jesus in the Black religious experience.

One other example will suffice. This hymn expresses the confident faith in God in time of trouble:

1. 'Tis faith supports my feeble soul
   In times of deep distress;
   When storms arise and billows roll,
   Great God, I trust thy grace.

2. Thy powerful arm still bears me up,
   Whatever grief befall;
   Thou art my life, my joy, my hope,
   And thou my all in all.

3. Bereft of friends, beset with foes,
   With dangers all around,
   To thee I all my fears disclose;
   In thee my help is found.

4. In every want, in every strait,
   To thee alone I fly;
   When other comforters depart,
   Thou art forever nigh.[24]

In general use, only two full stanzas would be sung since the singing of the entire hymn would be rather time-consuming. Often the indication of the last stanza to be sung is made by the congregation coming to its feet. Once the congregation is seated again, the "moaning" of a stanza rounds off the rendition.

It is incumbent upon those churches where Black meter music still lives that pains are taken to preserve this valuable music art form that is a genuine part of the continuum of the oral tradition of Black sacred music.

SUPPLEMENT—WORDS ONLY.

Mutual Aid.
C. M.

1 Try us, O God, and search the
   ground
Of every sinful heart:
Whate'er of sin in us is found,
O bid it all depart!

2 When to the right or left we stray,
Leave us not comfortless;
But guide our feet into the way
Of everlasting peace.

3 Help us to help each other, Lord,
Each other's cross to bear:
Let each his friendly aid afford,
And feel his brother's care.

4 Help us to build each other up,
Our little stock improve:
Increase our faith, confirm our hope,
And perfect us in love.

5 Up into thee, our living Head,
Let us in all things grow;
Till thou hast made us free indeed,
And spotless here below.

6 Then, when the mighty work is
   wrought,
Receive thy ready bride:
Give us in heaven a happy lot
With all the sanctified.

Everlasting Absence of God Intolerable.
C. M.   WATTS.

1 That awful day will surely come,—
Th' appointed hour makes haste,—
When I must stand before my Judge,
And pass the solemn test.

2 Thou lovely Chief of all my joys,
Thou Sovereign of my heart,
How could I bear to hear thy voice
Pronounce the sound, "Depart!"

3 O, wretched state of deep despair,
To see my God remove,
And fix my dreadful station where
I must not taste his love!

4 Jesus, I throw my arms around,
And hang upon thy breast;
Without one gracious smile from
   thee,
My spirit cannot rest.

5 O, tell me that my worthless name
Is graven on thy hands;
Show me some promise in thy book,
Where my salvation stands.

And Are We Yet Alive.
S. M. D.

1 And are we yet alive,
   And see each other's face?
Glory and praise to Jesus give
   For his redeeming grace!
Preserved by power Divine
   To full salvation here,
Again in Jesus' praise we join,
   And in his sight appear.

2 What troubles have we seen,
   What conflicts have we passed,
Fightings without, and fears within,
   Since we assembled last!
But out of all the Lord
   Hath brought us by his love;
And still he doth his help afford,
   And hides our life above.

3 Then let us make our boast
   Of his redeeming power,
Which saves us to the uttermost,
   Till we can sin no more:
Let us take up the cross,
   Till we the crown obtain;
And gladly reckon all things loss,
   So we may Jesus gain.

SUPPLEMENT—WORDS ONLY.

Prayer for Grace in Trial.
C. M.
URWICK'S COL.

1 Father of all our mercies, thou
   In whom we move and live,
   Hear us in heaven, thy dwelling,
      now;
   And answer, and forgive.

2 When, harassed by ten thousand
      foes,
   Our helplessness we feel,
   O, give the weary soul repose,
   The wounded spirit heal.

3 When dire temptations gather round,
   And threaten or allure,
   By storm or calm, in thee be found
   A refuge strong and sure.

4 When age advances, may we grow
   In faith, in hope, and love,
   And walk in holiness below
   To holiness above.

Another Soldier Gone.
S. M.
REV. B. J. PERKINS

1 Another soldier gone
   To get a great reward;
   He fought the fight and kept the
      faith
   And now gone home to God.

2 He fought until he fell
   Upon the battle field,
   And then he heard the General say,
   "Lay down your sword and
      shield."

3 His soul has gone to God
   The earth has claimed its own,
   And now he's shouting 'round the
      throne,
   While we are left to mourn.

4 Some day we'll meet again,
   Our loved ones gone before;
   Some day we'll reach that happy
      land,
   Where parting is no more.

Love to the Lord Declared.
C. M.

1 I love the Lord: he heard my cries,
   And pitied every groan:
   Long as I live, when troubles rise,
   I'll hasten to his throne.

2 I love the Lord: he bowed his ear,
   And chased my grief away:
   Oh, let my heart no more despair
   While I have breath to pray.

3 The Lord beheld me sore distressed;
   He bade my pains remove;
   Return, my soul, to God, thy rest,
   For thou hast known his love.

Christ Superior to Moses.
C. M.

1 How strong thine arm is, mighty
      God,
   Who would not fear thy name?
   Jesus, how sweet thy graces are,
   Who would not love the Lamb?

2 He has done more than Moses did:
   Our Prophet and our King,
   From bonds of hell has freed our
      souls
   And taught our lips to sing.

3 In the Red Sea, by Moses' hand,
   The Egyptian host was drowned;
   But his own blood hides all our sins,
   And guilt no more is found.

4 When through the desert Israel
      went,
   With manna they were fed:
   Our Lord invites us to his flesh,
   And calls it living bread.

SUPPLEMENT—WORDS ONLY.

5 Moses beheld the promised land,
    Yet never reached the place:
But Christ shall bring his followers
        home,
    To see his Father's face.

6 Then will our love and joy be full,
    And feel a warmer flame,
And sweeter voices tune the song
    Of Moses and the Lamb.

The Christian Race.
C. M.   DODDRIDGE.

1 Awake, my soul: stretch every nerve,
    And press with vigor on;
A heavenly race demands thy zeal,
    And an immortal crown.

2 A cloud of witnesses around
    Hold thee in full survey;
Forget the steps already trod,
    And onward urge thy way.

3 'Tis God's all-animating voice
    That calls thee from on high;
'Tis his own hand presents the prize
    To thine uplifted eye;—

4 That prize, with peerless glories
        bright,
    Which shall new lustre boast,
When victors' wreaths and mon-
        archs' gems
    Shall blend in common dust.

The Day Is Past and Gone.
S. M.

1 The day is past and gone,
    The evening shades appear;
Oh, may we all remember well
    The night of death draws near.

2 We lay our garments by,
    Upon our beds to rest;
So death will soon dis-robe us all
    Of what is here possessed.

3 Lord, keep us safe this night,
    Secure from all our fears;
May Angels guard us while we sleep,
    Till morning light appears.

4 And when we early rise
    And view th' unwearied sun,
May we set out to win the prize,
    And after glory run.

5 And when our days are past
    And we from time remove,
Oh may we in thy bosom rest,
    The bosom of thy love.

Funeral Hymn.
C. M.

1 Hark! from the tombs a doleful
        sound!
    My ears attend the cry;
"Ye living men, come view the
        ground,
    Where you must shortly lie.

2 "Princes, this clay must be your bed,
    In spite of all your towers;
The tall, the wise, the reverend head
    Must lie as low as ours."

3 Great God, is this our certain doom?
    And are we still secure?
Still walking downward to the tomb,
    And yet prepare no more!

4 Grant us the power of quickening
        grace,
    To fit our souls to fly;
Then, when we drop this dying
        flesh,
    We'll rise above the sky.

"What a Friend We Have in Jesus" 6

Hymns of Improvisation

The music of this section has been arbitrarily titled "Hymns of Improvisation." Within the Black Church community they are known as "gospelized hymns" because they evidence the imprint of the Black religious experience in the rhythm-style performance with which they are rendered. However, from a historical point of view, there is some error in the use of that label, for "gospel" in the context of the Black Church did not appear until after 1920. The body of music under scrutiny here was in broad use by the beginning of the twentieth century, and the use of these hymns with a Black imprint was widespread. The verbiage "gospelized hymns" developed, understandably, in a lay person's attempt to distinguish the style of rendition. Thus, for historical accuracy, the author has settled on the term "Hymns of Improvisation" for the purposes of this study.

This body of hymns is almost entirely Euro-American in origin and authorship. With the exception of C. A. Tindley, Lucie Campbell, and a few others, not many Black poets gave themselves to hymn form in the technical sense. Two parallel and directly related circumstances greatly influenced the use of these Euro-American hymns in the worship services of the Black community: the accelerated growth of the Black Church as an institution and the sharp increase in literacy that came during the period just before the turn of the century. As Black Christians developed their own unique religious institutions, they borrowed from around them and incorporated whatever was useful for their purposes. Clergy-led organized congregations, church buildings, choirs, and hymnbooks made their appearance on the expanding Black religious scene. The historical period of these hymns is 1875 to 1930. The Fisk Jubilee Singers during the early part of this period had popularized the original music of Black people, the Spirituals, and early development of the "visible church" had made good use of Dr. Watts, the Wesleys, and others in developing the Black meter music tradition. As the twentieth century drew near, the growing literacy among the former slaves manifested itself. One clear evidence, religiously, is the Euro-American hymn that became part and parcel of Black hymnody. The meter music tradition did not require a high level of literacy; now, with literacy the use of hymns, without "lining" the words every two lines, was possible.

The Black religious community, increasingly urban, took the Euro-American hymn tunes and gave them an exaggerated measure, syncopation, and rendered them in the "surge" style closely akin to their musical imprint on the meter music tradition. This "improvisation" was augmented by either piano or organ, and after the turn of the century both. Once Black folks laid hands on the Euro-American hymns and gave to them the musical overlay common to the Spiritual and the Black meter music tradition, the hymns would be forever changed. This fact is obvious when the original hymn tune is sung "straight," or precisely as the musical notation demands, and then is compared with a rendition by any random body of Black worshipers who have never seen one another before. The lyric texts are identical, but the performance, musically, is of another kind altogether. It is at this juncture of performance that the oral tradition introduces itself again; the "standard," or well-known, Euro-American hymns require no special instruction for Black rendition. The Black religious community instinctively knows how to sing them. The mode of singing is common to the Black religious experience and is passed from one generation to another via an oral tradition in Black sacred music.

The Period of Hymns of Improvisation—1875–1930

The Time Bar, Figure 8, indicates clearly that the samples of Black sacred music, chosen for this study, did not develop in clearly marked time periods. In each instance, there is considerable overlapping. The

FIGURE 8

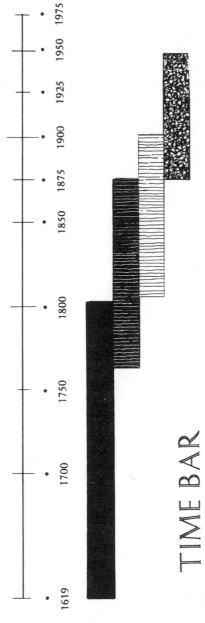

TIME BAR

Black Sacred Music

Period of Development & Dominance

1619   1700   1750   1800   1850   1875   1900   1925   1950   1975

SLAVES UTTERANCES/Moans, Chants, Cries for Deliverance

SPIRITUALS/Faith-Songs, Sorrow Songs, Plantation Hymns, etc.

METER MUSIC/Watts, Wesley, Sankey et al.

HYMNS OF IMPROVISATION/Euro-American hymns with "beat"

17795

Hymns of Improvisation, as we have described them above, came into use during the period of the ascendancy of the Black meter music tradition. A brief survey of the earlier part of the historical period of the Hymns of Improvisation was made in chapter 5. However, one aspect of that period (1875–1900) impinges directly on this style of Black sacred music, and some brief comments in this regard may prove helpful.

Post-Reconstruction to the Turn of the Century

In the preface to the first edition of John Hope Franklin's classic, *From Slavery to Freedom,* the author cites his focus as "tracing the interaction of the Negro and the American environment."[1] Black people were affected by the general flow of American history and responded to that flow of circumstances, no small part of that response being registered in their religious practice of which a central portion was their music.

The Period of post-Reconstruction referred to above had disastrous effects on the life of Black people with one single exception—the improved educational status of the freedmen.[2]

The path of education for Negroes at all levels was aided greatly by the philanthropic mood that filled the breach left by the withdrawal of the Freedmen's Bureau. The two chief aids to Negro education in the South were the denominational boards that did so much to establish schools for the former slaves and the age of philanthropy that came hard on the heels of Reconstruction. Franklin notes, "It was an age of philanthropy, and Negro education benefited substantially."[3]

The American Missionary Association of the Congregational Church was a strong advocate of education for Negroes, and Baptists dotted the South with schools through their Home Mission Society. Methodists, Presbyterians, Episcopalians, and Catholics joined the fray, and each of the major Negro denominations established both secondary schools and colleges.[4] The evidence of the latter was observable in many quarters of the South as late as the mid-forties. In the rural areas particularly, the school was next to the church in the Black community. Many of the secondary schools for Negroes gained public tax-based support only when the breeze of desegregation began to blow faintly in the 1950s.

The preeminence of the drive for education among Negroes during this period helps to explain the prominence of Booker T. Washington, whose accommodation to political, economic, and social disfranchisement of Blacks made possible the period's general acceptance of the concept of Negro education.[5] The growing Black Church, as an institution, was unrivaled as the center of Negro socialization, and the impact of the period surfaced in church life with a remarkable increase in literacy. At emancipation, "about one in every twenty Negroes could read and write. [At the turn of the century] thirty-five years later, more than one out of every two could read and write."[6] The rise in literacy was nothing less than dramatic. The children of parents who made untold sacrifices for their schooling were, in turn, helped with their "letters" by these same children. Elderly Blacks today confess that much of their early schooling centered in the Bible and the Sears and Roebuck catalogue. In turn, the increased literacy facilitated the introduction of hymnbooks into church services, and Black folks and Euro-American hymns were joined together.

The rise of literacy among Blacks profoundly affected the next development in the arena of Black sacred music. The ability to read brought the Euro-American hymns into the focus of Black Church life and left upon them the indelible imprint of the Black religious experience.

The Turn of the Century to World War I—1900–1914

The turn of the century in the United States gave clear evidence that this country had survived the paroxysms of the Civil War, and, in less than a quarter century, had emerged as one of the most highly industrialized nations in the world. The domestic strife that centered primarily in the "Negro question" did not deter this fledgling nation from practicing New World imperialism just as her counterparts in Europe were practicing colonialism. While the Berlin conference (1884–1885) was dividing Africa, the U. S. was busy putting together its own empire of darker peoples. In swift succession, by hook or by crook, the Hawaiian Islands, the Philippines, Cuba, Puerto Rico, the Virgin Islands, the Dominican Republic, and Haiti fell under the spell of American domination, either by outright acquisition or through the influence of the Yankee dollar.[7] The U.S.A. had joined the small circle of the great powers of the world, dominating other nations.

The mood of the country at the turn of the century was one of optimism and prosperity, and plenty seemed just around the corner for everyone. Even the hopes of Negro Americans seemed justified. The disfranchisement in the South and the economic difficulties appeared manageable. Besides, Teddy Roosevelt was president! The hope was short-lived. The hopes and dreams of Blackamericans were all but ashes by the time the sword-rattling of World War I had begun.

The Black community in America, most of it in the South, had managed to develop despite the ups and downs of Reconstruction and post-Reconstruction. By the close of the nineteenth century there had been some significant developments in spite of white hostility, South and North. The former slaves had experienced steady growth in their religious institutions following the phenomenal growth after the Civil War. National denominational bodies had been formed, and along with the individual churches, they were plugged into the herculean efforts of educating the Negroes that were abroad in the land. Their social and cultural growth proceeded, though forced to do so outside the larger American community. Much of this growth was centered in the Black Church but not limited to the church. Fraternal societies had sprung up all over the South and became the precursors of the great insurance companies. Before 1914, fifty-five Black banks had been chartered,[8] and the internal development of the Black community was chronicled by numerous historical works and autobiographies that detailed indirectly the role of the former slave in this republic. A few Negro newspapers were begun in principal cities with the stated purpose of agitating for Negro rights as citizens. The obstacles that confronted the Black people at the close of the nineteenth century in no way dissuaded them from trying to make it in the U.S. just like other Americans. Thus, there was some sound basis for being hopeful, though such an attitude was of little avail.

The most pronounced change in the life of the Black community since the Emancipation Proclamation began to take place at just about the turn of the century. The industrialization of America had a concomitant effect on the agrarian economy of the South that was all but disastrous to Black people. Following the Civil War, whatever adjustments the newly freed slave made were principally rural adjustments. As an infrequent landowner and a frequent share-cropper, the bulk of the Black population remained for the most part in the rural area. As industrialization deepened in America, the Black community was jarred loose from the land and, just like other Americans so affected, turned to the urban centers of the South and North to seek better economic opportunities. As city life rose in America generally, so rose the incidence of the large Black community within the city.

The shift of great numbers of Blacks to the urban centers of the North and South created its own peculiar problems. Employment opportunities were thin, and the number of Blacks coming to those centers far exceeded the number of jobs available. With the influx of Blacks into the cities housing restrictions were passed into law, designating "White" blocks and "Negro" blocks.

This sharp shift in population into the cities only intensified the hostility toward Blacks that was always present, North as well as South. However, hardly anyone would have predicted the spate of racial violence that came close on the heels of this major population shift in the Black community. During the first year of the new century, more than one hundred lynchings were reported, and by World War I, the number had risen to eleven hundred. It was during this same period that America suffered an epidemic of race riots. More than anything else, race riots instilled in Negroes a great sense of insecurity during this period. The badge of color too often was the mark of "open season" on Black people. Statesboro and Atlanta, Georgia, Brownsville, Texas, and Springfield, Illinois, were the worst, while others erupted in alleged bastions of liberality like New York and Philadelphia.[9]

In reaction to the wanton mayhem inflicted indiscriminately on the Black community during this savage era in American history, the leader of the emerging Black elitists, W. E. B. Du Bois, convened what was to become the Niagara Movement. This group insisted upon "freedom of speech and criticism, manhood suffrage, the abolition of all distinctions based on race, the recognition of the basic principles of human brotherhood, and respect for the working man."[10] Following the Springfield riots, outraged whites joined with a nucleus of the Niagara Movement and formed the National Association for the Advancement of Colored People. It was formally chartered in 1910.[11] Segregation became the chief foil of the NAACP, along with its long quest for federal antilynching legislation. In its early papers, the NAACP planned to work at widening the industrial opportunities for Blacks but found little time to work in this area. In 1911, the crisis in economic affairs among Blacks led to the founding of the National Urban League. The League saw as its chief and central task "to assist newly arrived Negroes in their problems of adjustment in the urban centers" and "to open new opportunities for Negroes in industry. . . . "[12] However, as World War I approached, science and reason in the matter of race seemed no match for passion and prejudice. It was a difficult hour for Black people to be hopeful about the future.

World War I to the Great Depression—1914–1930

When the great powers of Europe plunged into World War I, Blacks in America were all but demoralized. Many Negro Americans had lived through the disappointment of post-Reconstruction. The new century had seemed to hold great promise as did the new president, Theodore Roosevelt. As far as the Black community and its vital interests were concerned, both were flops. Lynching continued unabated, and the rash of serious race riots made the plight of Blackamericans tenuous indeed. A glimmer of hope flickered in the election of Woodrow Wilson, to whom large numbers of Blacks defected from their traditional Republicanism, but that was short-lived, too. More segregation measures were introduced at the federal level during the first year of Wilson's presidency than had ever been submitted in the history of the nation.[13] Even Wilson's protestations of evenhanded justice could do little to neutralize the deep-seated and vehement White versus Black hostility. Sporadic mayhem and murder were inflicted upon Negroes, in both the South and the North, and generally, White perpetrators escaped with full impunity. Law and order did not exist for the victims of White racist anger and hatred. Then came the *coup de grace* to Black folks' down-turned fortunes: Booker T. Washington died in 1915. The one strong and respected voice which had secured some concessions in the interest of social uplift was stilled. This was the plight of Blackamericans as the war in Europe was pursued in earnest.

The signs of the Black community's desperate circumstance were clear, and the more spirited leaders of Negro affairs convened the Amenia Conference in 1916.[14] Unity was the theme, and just before America entered the war, these distinguished leaders agreed that the priority agenda for Negro Americans must include enfranchisement of the Negro, the abolition of lynching, and strict enforcement of the laws protecting civil liberties.

Before much of anything could be done, the *Lusitania* was sunk, and America became a full participant in World War I, ostensibly "to make the world safe for democracy." Making the United States safe for Blacks, as an item of severe domestic crisis, was shelved for the duration of the war.

To the credit of all Black people, Negro Americans set aside the heavy burden of their disappointments with America and gave almost total support to the war effort. One-third of the American expeditionary forces that served in Europe were Black. In combat and work battalions, Blacks distinguished themselves despite the overall segregated policies of the armed services. Back home, despite the enforced income status, Negroes gave admirable support to the international conflict, especially through the purchase of Liberty Bonds. No small part of the Black people's enthusiastic support to their troubled nation was filling the great manpower void in the industrial North, created by the war and the sharp decline of foreign immigration. The economy of the South was aggravated by the onslaught of the boll weevil in 1915 and 1916. The natural disaster of floods and the human disaster of rampant injustice congealed with the other forces already mentioned to launch a major population shift of Blacks to the North. By the end of 1918, more than one million Blacks were seeking a new life above the Mason-Dixon line; this estimate may be exaggerated, however.[15] One positive aspect of this sharp shift in population was the relatively new opportunity for Blacks to enter industrial employment and, in turn, relieve the crucial manpower shortage mentioned above.

After the armistice was signed, Black soldiers were received with great enthusiasm all across the country except in the intransigent South. Great parades were held in New York, Chicago, and Buffalo. These heroes came home to establish their demands for first-class citizenship. The democracy and freedom they had tasted abroad meant nothing if there were now no freedom and democracy at home.

They returned to a United States, a nation anxious to return to peace-time normalcy—a bad omen for Black people. Within a year of the end of the war, the Ku Klux Klan, which numbered only a few thousand in 1918, grew to more than 100,000 members committed against "Negroes, Japanese and other orientals, Roman Catholics, Jews, and all foreign-born persons." [16] The summer of 1919, the year of the Black veterans' return, was dubbed by James Weldon Johnson "The Red Summer." [17] It marked the greatest period of interracial violence and terror the nation had ever known. Twenty-five race riots took place between June and December. The significant difference in these racial conflicts was that no longer was the Negro wont to absorb the violence inflicted by his tormentors; Black men demonstrated a willingness to fight and die in their own defense. The prospect of race war was at hand with this new ingredient injected into America's most severe social problem.

Claude McKay caught the temper of the moment in the Black psyche:

> If we must die—let it not be like hogs
> Hunted and penned in an inglorious spot,
> While round us bark the mad and hungry dogs,
> Making their mock at our accursed lot.
> If we must die—oh, let us nobly die,
> So that our precious blood may not be shed
> In vain; then even the monsters we defy
> Shall be constrained to honor us though dead!
> Oh, Kinsmen! We must meet the common foe;
> Though far outnumbered, let us show us brave,
> And for their thousand blows deal one death-blow!
> What though before us lies the open grave?
> Like men we'll face the murderous, cowardly pack,
> Pressed to the wall, dying, but fighting back! [18]

These were the circumstances of the Black community as they drifted into the Roaring Twenties toward the Great Depression. The decade following "The Red Summer" saw the rise of the Garvey movement, assessed by Franklin as the only grass-roots movement organized among Black people. The eminent historian concludes that despite the claims of several millions in his "Back to Africa" movement, "widespread interest in Garvey's program was more a protest against the anti-Negro reaction of the post-war period than an approbation of the fantastic schemes of the Negro leader." [19]

The period immediately following the war saw two things: the NAACP mount a valiant but futile struggle to secure federal anti-lynching legislation and the gradual emergence of Father Divine. As bad as things were for Black folks, the worst was yet to come. The Great Depression was just around the corner.

Social Significance of the Hymns of Improvisation

During the fifty-odd-year period that the Hymns of Improvisation came to broad use in the Black religious experience, two chief social factors were of great influence. The rise of literacy and the urbanization of the Black population produced profound changes in the religious life of Blackamericans as well as sharply affecting their life-style in general. Our concern here is to note as far as possible how the change in their sociological setting was reflected in Black people's religious practice and, more particularly, how changes, if any, are observable in their musical expression. The common rule of thumb is as applicable here as during any other period: The Black Church, as an institution in the Black community, registers directly and indirectly what is happening, good and bad, to Black people. Since music remains central in the religious life and practice of Black folk, a reasonably accurate reading can be made.

The two chief influences mentioned above—the rise of literacy and the urbanization of the Negro—had parallel and interlocking effects on Black church life. They are discussed separately only for the sake of analysis. It is perfectly obvious that the great movement of Blacks to urban centers would necessarily change the rural posture of Black religious life to one that was more reflective of the process of urbanization.

It might be recalled that during this period when Euro-American hymns came into Black church circles, there were two population shifts: the first, induced by economic circumstances, saw Blacks migrating from the rural South to the urban South; the second population shift was induced by the manpower exigencies of World War I, which saw a major population shift from the rural *and* urban South to the urban North. The end product of both population moves was a greatly increased number of Blacks in urban centers, North and South. The presence of Negroes in American cities changed markedly the configuration of Black church life and style. Previous to this period under consideration, the developing religious life and institutions were rural and semirural by demographic necessity. Black folks were not in the cities. These two population shifts changed that, and the church reflected that change.

The concentration of Blacks in urban areas led to congregations of greater size. In spite of their meager means, collectively their economic strength became more formidable. Thus the period of population shifts gave impetus to the development of the urban church milieu among Blacks as well as Whites. The increased number of sizable and impressive church structures within urban centers was increasingly patterned after the observable religious life of the dominant society. Physically, Black churches became auditorium and sanctuary oriented. Thus, in sharp contrast to the simple needs of rural-style worship that, at best, was intermittent, the church life of Blacks in the cities became an every-week affair. In the rural areas, one-Sunday- and two-Sunday-a-month services were all that was possible with limited transportation and leadership. This latter circumstance prevails even today in rural areas, though with not as great frequency as in years past.

The larger congregations, the changes in physical structures in arrangements and size encouraged the introduction of pianos and, later, organs. The advent of the hymnbook was at hand, followed closely with choirs and directors. Black folks, largely more literate than they had ever been before in their history, were not impervious to what was going on in the churches of the White community, and this period of Black church history clearly reflects that influence at this point. Thus, larger churches (in comparison to the rural experience), hymnbooks, instruments, choirs, and directors became the benchmarks of the Black Church's steady growth and development.

The rise in literacy among Blacks obviously contributed to the changes cited above. This is not to assert that literacy was universal, but only to indicate that the sharp rise in literacy among Blacks[20] manifested itself clearly in the goals of the developing religious life of the oppressed community. It was unlikely that churches would invest sizable amounts of money in hymnbooks and choirs and pianos and/or organs unless a goodly number of its members were literate to some degree. This underscores the phenomenon of urbanization among Blacks and the impact it had in the religious life of the Black community.

There was another index present that had interlocking significance. The shift in population to the cities, particularly during World War I, provided Blacks with their first real opportunities at industrial employment. Though the opportunities were not always broadly available, they made possible an income level in the Black community that it had not known before. In the urban centers of the South, personal service employment, along with the small Negro-directed businesses, had dominated the Negro economy. The point is that from whatever source money was earned, a sizable portion found its way into the most popular and populous enterprise in the Black community—the Black Church.

It was during this stage of Black Church development that the Euro-American hymns came into broad use. As long as Blacks were largely illiterate, the hymnbook did not have much of a chance. The rise of literacy opened the door, and the concomitant influences of urbanization cultivated the use of print-oriented church music. No small help was given by the increasing presence of choirs, pianos, organs, and directors, all of which gave evidence of a growing dollar strength of the Black Church as an institution.

The introduction of the hymnbook into Black worship services required some gradual adjustments. It has been mentioned that not *everyone* was literate; thus, choirs *led* hymns until the hymns became sufficiently familiar for them to be used congregationally. The use of hymns was relegated to use in the "formal service" at the beginning of this period, and the meter music and to some degree the Spirituals were reserved for the preservice "devotions," prayer meetings, and revivals. The very nature and character of the Euro-American hymns and the basic requirements for their use—instruments and literacy of some sort—were a social statement in themselves, indicating the degree of urbanization and physical development in the Black Church enterprise. The Black Church was rapidly establishing itself as the central force in the affairs of the Black community. After the turn of the century, once the NAACP and the Urban League were formed, much of the organizational development was aided and abetted by Black churches. They became an indispensable network of communication and support for anything of interest to Black people.

All that has gone before must be evaluated in the light of the hard realities. Black Church life demonstrated definite signs of growth (hymnbook worship) in spite of America's continuing disregard for the civil and human rights of its Black citizenry. The most startling phenomenon is that once hymnbook worship became an integral part of Black Church life, it was not long before the Black community put its indelible print on that which was distinctly Euro-American in origin. This is not to say that at no time did Blacks make use of Euro-American hymns as they are musically notated. It is altogether likely and probable that when hymnbooks were first introduced into Black worship services, the musical notations were followed slavishly. However, the oral tradition from Mother Africa has remained persistent, and with the recurring disappointments of this period, the author would hazard the guess that imperceptibly Blacks reverted to their natural musical idiom of rhythm and beat. The message of the Euro-American hymn poems was universal, but for appropriation's sake they had to be transposed into Black musical idiom, familiar to the Black religious experience. The change was as much a reaction to "white folks' ways" as it was to "white folks' singing." The Euro-American hymns in Black religious life were adapted by Black rhythm and Black improvisation in order that they would be useful. In the section following, we shall take a summary look at those hymns which have had broadest use in the Black religious community and note some of the more pronounced themes that relate to the Black condition.

Profile of the Hymns of Improvisation

The use of Euro-American hymns during this period in question reflects the steady and measurable development of the Black religious community in particular and the larger community in general. It may be helpful at this point to review and narrow sufficiently the definition of the music of which we speak.

The "Hymns of Improvisation" make up that body of music that is almost exclusively Euro-American in origin and authorship. This grouping does not include all Euro-American hymns; only those that historically have found frequent "improvised" use in the Black religious experience have been considered. This presumes and recognizes that some use has been made in Black worship of Euro-

American hymns *without* the "improvisation" of our concern here. Most Black Presbyterians and United Methodists probably sing Euro-American hymns exactly like their White counterparts. Black Christians, in response to their religious, psychic, and social needs in America, were selective in their use of Euro-American hymns. Thus, for the most part, we are dealing only with Euro-American hymns whose message of hope and inspiration spoke to Black Christians and whose original musical and poetic forms lent themselves to Black "improvisation." The Black people's sociological climate during this period of their American experience had its clear influence on that selection.

The authorship of the hymns frequently used in the Black religious experience bridges a time span that stretches from "Praise God, from Whom All Blessings Flow" (1692) to "In the Garden" (1912). It does not appear that Euro-American hymns of any special period had particular appeal. Blacks, however, always manifested a special liking of "Dr. Watts" tunes. Whatever the choice, the Black religious community, in its oppression, did not make random use of this new music. That which became most frequently used reflected the Black religious community's reaction and response to their social circumstance. It must be added, that at the same time that Black Christians were being selective about the music that suited their circumstance, the mere use of Euro-American hymns evidenced the impact of mainstream Christianity on Black church life. Inevitably, the urbanization of the Negro and the rise of literacy in the ranks led to some imitation of what they observed in the religious life of the dominant society. The use of Euro-American hymns was a part of that inevitable imitation and influence.

It is not the intention of this writer to suggest that the use of "improvised" hymns ended with the rise of the Gospel era. Many of them took on an additional improvisation, and, generally, broad use is still made of this style of Black sacred music. Aretha Franklin's record-breaking album *Amazing Grace* included several "improvised" Euro-American hymns.[21] In addition to the title song, "God Will Take Care of You," "What a Friend We Have in Jesus," and "Never Grow Old" appear and are variations on an old theme of Black improvisation.

On the adjoining pages there is a rather broad and extensive listing

Hymns of Improvisation
Comparative Listing Showing Author and Date of Authorship

Title	Author	Group
Stand Up, Stand Up for Jesus	George Duffield	2
Praise God, from Whom All Blessings Flow	Thomas Ken	1
Let All the People Praise Thee	(Mrs.) C. Morris	
I Love Thy Kingdom Lord	Timothy Dwight	1
O For A Thousand Tongues to Sing	Charles Wesley	1
Abide With Me! Fast Falls the Eventide	H. F. Lyte	2
O God Our Help In Ages Past	Isaac Watts	1
God Moves In A Mysterious Way	William Cowper	1
*Guide Me, O Thou Great Jehovah	William Williams	2
When I Survey the Wondrous Cross	Isaac Watts	1
In the Cross of Christ I Glory	J. Bowring	
Alas! and Did My Savior Bleed?	Isaac Watts	1
Dark Was the Night	Anonymous	1
Christ Arose!	Robert Lowry	2
Christ, the Lord is Risen Today	Charles Wesley	1
I Know That My Redeemer Lives	Charles Wesley	1
How Sweet the Name of Jesus Sounds	John Newton	1
O How I Love Jesus		
Come Thou Fount of Every Blessing	Robert Robinson	1
*No, Not One	Johnson Oatman	3
*Jesus Keep Me Near the Cross	F. J. Van Alstyne	3
The Name of Jesus	W. C. Martin	3
*There Is a Name I Love to Hear	F. Whitfield	3
Majestic Sweetness Sits Enthroned	S. Stennett	1
Holy Ghost With Light Divine	A. Reed	
Come, Holy Spirit Heavenly Dove	Isaac Watts	1
Come, Thou Almighty King	Charles Wesley	1
Holy, Holy, Holy, Lord God Almighty	Reginald Heber	2
We Praise Thee O God	W. P. MacKay	2
Wonderful Words of Life	P. P. Bliss	
Not All the Blood of Beasts	Isaac Watts	1
"Go Preach My Gospel," Saith the Lord	Isaac Watts	1

*All-time favorites   ☐ Jesus Theme

Title	Author	Group
*There is a Fountain Filled With Blood	William Cowper	1
Come Ye Disconsolate	Thomas Moore	2
Only Trust Him	J. H. Stockton	
Lift Him Up	Johnson Oatman	3
Hark! the Herald Angels Sing	Charles Wesley	1
Silent Night, Holy Night	Joseph Mohr	
Sweet By and By	S. F. Bennett	
Just Over in the Glory-Land	Jas. W. Acuff	3
Keep Me Every Day	F. L. Eiland	
We'll Understand It Better, By and By	C. A. Tindley	3
Is Thy Heart Right With God?	E. A. Hoffman	2
Come to Jesus	Anonymous	
In Evil Long I Took Delight	John Newton	1
*Father I Stretch My Hands to Thee	Charles Wesley	1
I Hear Thy Welcome Voice	Louis Hartsough	2
The Lord Raised Me	James Rowe	3
I Surrender All	J. W. Van De Venter	
Just As I Am	C. Elliott	2
I Heard the Voice of Jesus Say	H. L. Cox	3
There is Power in the Blood	J. W. T. Tobias	
I Am Coming to the Cross	W. H. MacDonald	3
Lead, Kindly Light	J. H. Newman	2
Savior, More Than Life To Me	F. J. Van Alstyne	3
Cling to His Hand	L. Highfield	2
I Hear the Savior Say	Elvina Hall	3
*My Hope is Built On Nothing Less	Edward Mote	2
Safe in the Arms of Jesus	F. J. Van Alstyne	3
Jesus Saves	Priscilla J. Owens	
The Lord Is My Shepherd	James Montgomery	2
Is Your All on the Altar?	E. A. Hoffman	2
Jesus Is Calling	Fanny J. Crosby	3
The Old Rugged Cross	George Bennard	3
Softly and Tenderly	Will L. Thompson	
Hiding In Thee	William O. Cushing	
Joy to the World	Isaac Watts	1

*All-time favorites   ☐ Jesus Theme

Title	Author	Group
We Three Kings of Orient Are	John H. Hopkins	
Almost Persuaded	P. P. Bliss	
Glory to His Name	E. A. Hoffman	2
O Love That Wilt Not Let Me Go	George Matheson	
Lead On, O King Eternal	E. W. Shurtleff	
Blest Be the Tie	John Fawcett	
Work, for the Night Is Coming	Annie L. Coghill	
Tis So Sweet to Trust in Jesus	Louisa M. R. Stead	
Sweet By and By	S. F. Bennett	
Where We'll Never Grow Old	Jas. C. Moore	
When They Ring the Golden Bells	Dion De Marbelle	
The Lily of the Valley		
When the Battle's Over	Isaac Watts	1
Are Ye Able, Said the Master	Earl Marlatt	
Peace Be Still	Mary A. Baker	
Be Still, My Soul	K. Von Schlegel, J. L. Borthwick	
My Father Is Rich in Houses and Land	Hattie E. Buell	
I Feel Like Going On	W. T. Dale	3
*Beams of Heaven, As I Go	C. A. Tindley	3
O Happy Day, That Fixed My Choice	Philip Doddridge	1
Ring the Bells of Heaven	Wm. O. Cushing	
Come Ye That Love the Lord	Isaac Watts	1
Fade, Fade Each Earthly Joy	Catherine Bona	2
I'm Glad Salvation's Free	Anonymous	
More Love to Thee O Christ	Elizabeth Prentiss	2
My Jesus I Love Thee	Anonymous	2
Never Alone	Anonymous	
Prayer is the Soul's Sincere Desire	J. Montgomery	2
From Every Stormy Wind That Blows	H. Stowell	2
*Sweet Hour of Prayer	W. W. Walford	2
*What A Friend We Have In Jesus	Jos. Scriven	2
The Lord Will Work Wonders Today	G. P. Hott	
Answer Us Now	Arthur Spooner	3
*I Must Tell Jesus	E. A. Hoffman	2
Every Prayer Will Find Its Answer	(Mrs.) Frank Breck	3

*All-time favorites ☐ Jesus Theme

Title	Author	Group
Thou My Everlasting Portion	Fanny Crosby	3
Oh For a Heart to Praise My God	Charles Wesley	1
O For A Faith That Will Not Shrink	W. H. Bathurst	2
O For A Closer Walk With God	Wm. Cowper	1
* Pass Me Not O Gentle Savior	F. J. Van Alstyne	3
* I Am Thine O Lord	F. J. Van Alstyne	3
How Tedious and Tasteless the Hours	John Newton	1
Is My Name Written There?	Robert Seagrave	
More About Jesus	E. E. Hewitt	2
More Like Jesus Would I Be	F. J. Van Alstyne	3
Will There Be Any Stars?	E. E. Hewitt	2
Jesus, Savior, Pilot Me	Edward Hopper	3
My Faith Looks Up To Thee	Ray Palmer	2
I Need Thee Every Hour	Annie S. Hawkes	3
Nearer My God to Thee	Sarah F. Adams	2
I gave My Life For Thee	F. R. Havergal	2
Take My Life and Let It Be	Frances Havergal	2
A Charge To Keep I Have	Charles Wesley	1
* At The Cross	Isaac Watts	1
Standing On The Promises	Kelso Carter	3
All I Need	Chas. P. Jones	3
Nothing Between	C. A. Tindley	3
* Higher Ground	Johnson Oatman	3
His Way With Thee	Cyrus Nusbaum	3
Wear A Crown	Isaac Watts	1
Must Jesus Bear the Cross Alone	G. N. Allen	2
Onward Christian Soldiers	S. Baring-Gould	3
* I'll Overcome, Some Day	C. A. Tindley	3
Yield Not to Temptation	H. R. Palmer	
Shall We Gather At the River?	Robert Lowry	3
* On Jordan's Stormy Banks I Stand	S. Stennett	1
Servant of God, Well Done	J. Montgomery	2
Why Do We Mourn Departing Friends	Isaac Watts	1
Where Shall I Be?	Chas. P. Jones	3
There's A Land That is Fairer Than Day	S. F. Bennett	

* All-time favorites   ◼ Jesus Theme

Title	Author	Group
I've Reached the Land of Corn and Wine	Edgar Rage	
Over the River Faces I See	J. W. Van De Venter	
The Unclouded Day	J. K. Alwood	
'Twill Be Glory	J. L. Dockery	3
There is a Land of Pure Delight	Isaac Watts	1
Take Hold the Life-Line	E. E. Rexford	3
Sing the Wondrous Love of Jesus	E. E. Hewitt	3
Faith of Our Fathers	Frederick W. Faber	
Mother's Prayers Have Followed Me	Lizzie DeArmond	3
Sunshine in the Soul	E. E. Hewitt	3
O Beautiful For Spacious Skies	Katherine Bates	3
God of Our Fathers, Whose Almighty Hand	Daniel Roberts	3
Battle Hymn of the Republic	Julia Howe	2
My Country 'Tis of Thee	Samuel Smith	2
It Pays to Serve Jesus		
If Jesus Goes With Me		
Nothing But the Blood		
O Thou In Whose Presence	Jos. Swain	
A New Name in Glory	C. Austin Miles	
Blessed Quietness	Mrs. M. P. Ferguson	
There is Power in the Blood	L. E. Jones	
Count Your Blessings	Johnson Oatman	3
When We All Get to Heaven	E. E. Hewitt	2
Living For Jesus	T. O. Chisholm	
Lead Me to Calvary	Jenney Hissey	
'Tis So Sweet to Trust in Jesus	Louisa Stead	
Sweeter As The Years Go By	Mrs. C. H. Morris	
He Lifted Me	Charles H. Gabriel	
Saved	J. P. Schofield	
Rescue the Perishing	Fanny Crosby	3
He Hideth My Soul	Fanny Crosby	3
Let Jesus Come into Your Heart	Mrs. C. H. Morris	
Since Jesus Came into My Heart	R. A. McDaniel	
Jesus is Calling	Fanny Crosby	3
Jesus is All the World to Me	Will Thompson	

*All-time favorites   ☐ Jesus Theme

Title	Author	Group
Jesus, I Come	W. T. Sleeper	
Life's Railway to Heaven	M. E. Abbey	3
My Soul Be On Thy Guard	George Heath	1
*Blessed Assurance	Fanny Crosby	3
I Love to Tell the Story	Katherine Hankey	3
Bringing in the Sheaves	Knowles Shaw	
Lord Speak to Me That I May Speak	Frances Havergal	3
Am I A Soldier of the Cross	Isaac Watts	1
Count on Me	E. E. Hewitt	3
Hark! the Voice of Jesus Calling	Daniel March	3
Jesus Calls Us	Mrs. Cecil Alexander	
O Master Let Me Walk With Thee	Washington Gladden	
How Firm A Foundation	George Keith	1
All the Way My Savior Leads Me	F. J. Van Alstyne	3
I'm Happy With Jesus Alone	Chas. P. Jones	3
We're Marching to Zion	Isaac Watts	1
When Peace Like a River	H. G. Spafford	2
Rock of Ages, Cleft for Me	A. M. Toplady	1
I Can Hear My Savior Calling	E. W. Blandly	
*Leaning On the Everlasting Arms	E. A. Hoffman	3
I'm Going Through With Jesus	Herbert Buffum	3
I'm Not Ashamed to Own My Lord	Isaac Watts	1
The Haven of Rest	H. L. Gilmour	
God Will Take Care of You	C. D. Martin	3
*Amazing Grace	John Newton	1
In the Garden	C. Austin Miles	3
My Loved Ones Are Waiting for Me	J. D. Vaughn	3
Jesus, Lover of My Soul	Charles Wesley	1
When I Can Read My Title Clear	Isaac Watts	1
Stand By Me	C. A. Tindley	3
The Church's One Foundation	S. J. Stone	3
Zion Stands With Hills Surrounded	Thomas Kelly	2
In All My Lord's Appointed Ways	John Small	
Break Thou the Bread of Life	Mary Lathbury	
What Are Those Soul-Reviving Strains	J. Montgomery	2

*All-time favorites   ☐ Jesus Theme

Title	Author	Group
Lord, I Hear of Showers of Blessings	E. Conder	3
Praise Him! Praise Him!	Fanny Crosby	3
Bring Them In	Alexcenah Thomas	3
Savior, Like A Shepherd Lead Us	Dorothy Thrupp	2
Brightly Beams Our Father's Mercy	P. P. Bliss	
Jesus Shall Reign Where'er the Sun	Isaac Watts	1
I'll Go Where You Want Me to Go	Mary Brown	3
Throw Out the Life-Line	E. S. Ufford	

*All-time favorites   ☐ Jesus Theme

of Euro-American hymns frequently used in Black religious life. The titles alone are suggestive of the kinds of needs the hymns filled. The listing is augmented (where possible) by the names of authors and a number coding which indicates in what period a particular hymn had its origin. Group 1 covers the period 1692–1800; Group 2, 1801–1865; and Group 3, 1866–1930. The grouping reflects, in a general way, three distinct historical periods in the life of the Black community that correspond to the development of their hymnody.

The tables indicate very clearly that authorship by period demonstrates hardly any pattern at all. It is fairly obvious that Group 3 is the largest, which is attributable to the fact that these hymns were written most recently. Of the 219 hymns included in these tables 45 were written between 1692 and 1800 (Group 1), 40 between 1801 and 1865 (Group 2), and 65 between 1866 and 1920. The remaining hymns could not be dated accurately according to the sources used.[22] The listing does reveal the lasting popularity and affection for "Dr. Watts" hymns. Several are carryovers from the meter music era, having received distinct hymn tunes at a date later than their authorship.

About one-half of the hymns listed have "Jesus themes," mirroring the centrality of Jesus in the Black religious experience. (The shading on the tables indicates these hymns with "Jesus themes.") Admittedly, the Jesus umbrella includes such topics as "Trust and Confidence," "Cross and Resurrection," "Praise and Adoration," but the fixation of the Black religious community on Jesus is widely known.

As in the music of Spirituals, the Jesus emphasis transmits a quality of intimacy and companionship that leaps the barrier of God's transcendence. The commonality of this theme—Jesus emphasis—runs throughout Black hymnody.

One-fourth of the hymns thematically expresses "Dependence on God," one-tenth "Praise and Adoration" and one-tenth "Death and Immortality." The remaining five percent is variously divided among other religious themes.

The musical representation that follows is illustrative of the technical aspects of improvisation. Figure 9a is the precise musical notation of "Jesus, Keep Me Near the Cross," a familiar and beloved hymn among most Blacks.[23] Figure 9b is an approximation of what happens musically when Black improvisation takes place. Note that the original 6/8 time is extended to an exaggerated measure, 9/8 time, syncopation ("ragged" time) is introduced, and melismatic slurs (surge-style) are added, note to note and phrase to phrase. These musical ingredients are apparent here and generally common to all Black-idiom music.

Henry H. Mitchell, in a thoughtful article on Black Improvisation, perceptively notes that there are three essentials operative in the improvisational process: *joy, a group experience,* and *a directing by the "spirit,"* aided by a familiarity with cultural skills.[24] All three are evident when a congregation in the Black folk tradition lifts its communal voice in song, following the lyrics of a Euro-American author, and by musical means of an oral tradition that persists until today makes a faith statement of its ultimate trust in God. There is very little in church life that can be more moving and powerful. The Hymns of Improvisation are another musical gift to the Christian family from the Black religious experience.

On the pages following are several all-time favorites of the Black religious community. Any of these Euro-American hymns would be immediately familiar and, in all likelihood, be sung as a Hymn of Improvisation. A mini-survey revealed that the first three—"What a Friend We Have in Jesus," "Jesus, Keep Me Near the Cross," and "Amazing Grace"—are universally the most popular, and any one of the three could be "number one."

FIGURE 9a

Near the Cross

FANNY J. CROSBY   WILLIAM H. DOANE

1. Je - sus, keep me near the cross— There a pre - cious foun - tain,

FIGURE 9b

What a Friend We Have in Jesus

(WHAT A FRIEND. 8s, 7s. D.)

Joseph Scriven, 1855.

C. C. Converse.

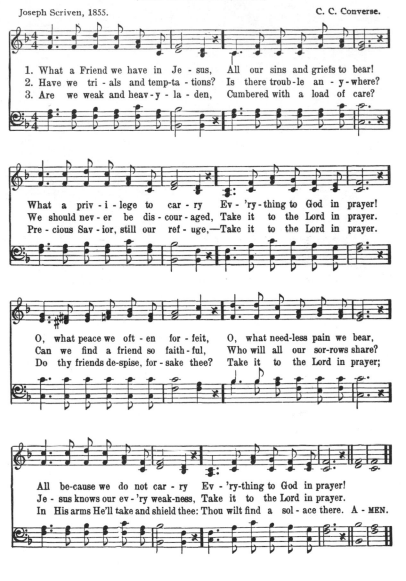

1. What a Friend we have in Je - sus, All our sins and griefs to bear!
2. Have we tri - als and temp-ta - tions? Is there troub-le an - y - where?
3. Are we weak and heav-y - la - den, Cumbered with a load of care?

What a priv - i - lege to car - ry Ev - 'ry-thing to God in prayer!
We should nev - er be dis - cour - aged, Take it to the Lord in prayer.
Pre - cious Sav - ior, still our ref - uge,—Take it to the Lord in prayer.

O, what peace we oft - en for - feit, O, what need-less pain we bear,
Can we find a friend so faith - ful, Who will all our sor-rows share?
Do thy friends de-spise, for - sake thee? Take it to the Lord in prayer;

All be-cause we do not car - ry Ev - 'ry-thing to God in prayer!
Je - sus knows our ev - 'ry weak-ness, Take it to the Lord in prayer.
In His arms He'll take and shield thee: Thou wilt find a sol - ace there. A - MEN.

Jesus, Keep Me Near the Cross

(NEAR THE CROSS. P. M.)

Frances Jane Van Alstyne, 1869.

W. H. Doane.

1. Je - sus, keep me near the cross; There a pre-cious foun-tain, Free to all, a
2. Near the cross, a trembling soul, Love and mer-cy found me; There the bright and
3. Near the cross! O Lamb of God, Bring its scenes be - fore me; Help me walk from
4. Near the cross I'll watch and wait, Hop-ing, trust-ing ev - er, Till I reach the

CHORUS.

healing stream. Flows from Calv'ry's mountain.
morning star Sheds its beams around me.   In the cross, in the cross, Be my glo-ry
day to day, With its shad-ow o'er me.
gold-en strand, Just be-yond the riv - er.

ev - er, Till the rap-tured soul shall find Rest be-yond the riv - er.   A-MEN.

Amazing Grace! How Sweet the Sound

(WILLA. C. M.)

John Newton.

Arr. by Dr. A. M. Townsend.

1. A - maz - ing grace! how sweet the sound That
2. 'Twas grace that taught my heart to fear, And
3. Through man - y dan - gers, toils and snares, I
4. The Lord has prom - ised good to me; His
5. Yes, when this heart and flesh shall fail, And
6. The earth shall soon dis - solve like snow, The
7. When we've been there ten thou - sand years, Bright

saved a wretch like me! I once was lost, but
grace my fears re - lieved; How pre - cious did that
have al - read - y come; 'Tis grace hath brought me
word my hope se - cures; He will my shield and
mor - tal life shall cease, I shall pos - sess, with-
sun for - bear to shine; But God, who called me
shin - ing as the sun, We've no less days to

now am found, Was blind, but now I see.
grace ap - pear The hour I first be - lieved.
safe thus far, And grace will lead me home.
por - tion be As long as life en - dures.
in the veil, A life of joy and peace.
here be - low, Will be for - ev - er mine.
sing God's praise Than when we first be - gun. A - MEN.

Guide Me, O Thou Great Jehovah

William Williams.   (8, 7, 4, 7.)   Dr. T. Hastings.

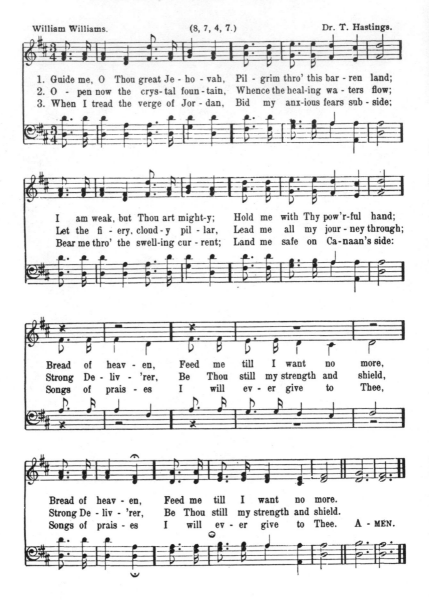

1. Guide me, O Thou great Je - ho - vah, Pil - grim thro' this bar - ren land;
2. O - pen now the crys - tal foun - tain, Whence the heal-ing wa - ters flow;
3. When I tread the verge of Jor - dan, Bid my anx-ious fears sub - side;

I am weak, but Thou art might-y; Hold me with Thy pow'r-ful hand;
Let the fi - er·y, cloud - y pil - lar, Lead me all my jour - ney through;
Bear me thro' the swell-ing cur - rent; Land me safe on Ca-naan's side:

Bread of heav - en, Feed me till I want no more.
Strong De - liv - 'rer, Be Thou still my strength and shield,
Songs of prais - es I will ev - er give to Thee,

Bread of heav - en, Feed me till I want no more.
Strong De - liv - 'rer, Be Thou still my strength and shield.
Songs of prais - es I will ev - er give to Thee. A - MEN.

Blessed Assurance

Fanny J. Crosby.

Mrs. J. F. Knapp.

1. Bless-ed as-sur-ance, Je-sus is mine! Oh, what a fore-taste of glo-ry di-vine! Heir of sal-va-tion, pur-chase of God, Born of His Spir-it, washed in His blood.

2. Per-fect sub-mis-sion, per-fect de-light, Vi-sions of rap-ture now burst on my sight, An-gels de-scend-ing, bring from a-bove Ech-oes of mer-cy, whis-pers of love.

3. Per-fect sub-mis-sion, all is at rest, I in my Sav-ior am hap-py and blest, Watching and wait-ing, look-ing a-bove, Filled with His good-ness, lost in His love.

REFRAIN.

This is my sto-ry, this is my song, Prais-ing my Sav-ior all the day long; This is my sto-ry, this is my song, Prais-ing my Sav-ior all the day long. A-MEN.

"The Lord Will Make 7
a Way Somehow!"

Gospel: Historic and Modern

The advent of Gospel music completed the full circle of Black musical expression on the North American continent. This study had traced the continuum of the oral tradition in Black sacred music that commenced with the creation of the Spiritual and all of its musical "cousins." The basically African Spiritual form influenced the meter music, which in turn colored the use of Euro-American hymns by Black Christians. The language of the latter two musical types was borrowed from the dominant society and revamped musically to suit the religious needs of the Black community. The Depression era produced another (musical) art form whose lyric and musical roots were in the Black religious experience—"Gospel."

Gospel music, in the words of Tony Heilbut, "good news and bad times,"[1] was spawned in the midst of the nation's worst economic crisis. The Gospel form evidenced the blues-jazz mode from the so-called secular world and rejoined old roots almost forgotten.

Today, the Gospel umbrella in its most advanced form embraces the spiritual idiom, contemporary social comment, elements of meter music style, and, when needed, the lyrics of Euro-American hymns. The composite result is a form of urban spiritual, a song of faith which rallies the hope and aspiration of the faithful in the face of devastating social conditions.

Thomas A. Dorsey is considered the "Father of Gospel Music." It was he who gave it its name—*gospel* music—in contradistinction to the gospel hymns used in the crusades of Dwight Lyman Moody and Ira David Sankey.[2] Horace Boyer, in his 1974 essay on Dorsey, is explicit on this distinction:

A cursory glance at these songs will show that they are in fact "gospel hymns": strictly organized, standard Protestant hymns of eight bars to the verse and eight bars to the chorus, with no provisions for the improvisation so much a part of Prof. Dorsey's song, nor the textual attention given to such matters as blessings, sorrows, woes and the joys of the "after-life," nor the Africanisms which really constitute gospel music—the altered scale degrees and the intricate rhythm which separates this music from all others.[3]

Gospel music, at bottom, is religious folk music that is clearly identifiable with the social circumstance of the Black community in America. The authenticity of folkways and folk expressions (including music) can be gauged by how closely they mirror the experience of the group. Gospel music does precisely that, in very much the same manner as does its early predecessor the Spiritual. Gospel music, then, is an individual expression of a collective predicament within a religious context. Dorsey says very much the same things in an interview in 1974. "Somebody once wrote that I see gospel music 'as meaning a message of good tidings expounded by one who has walked the path of trouble and hard times. . . .'"[4]

Boyer, in the same essay quoted earlier, says that Gospel songs can only be categorized by one standard—*tempo:* "Any gospel song, regardless of the text, tempo or mode, can be performed as a 'slow,' 'without rhythm' or 'fast' song—the only possible way to group gospel songs."[5] Boyer is fundamentally correct, but any historical survey of the Gospel phenomenon will reveal distinctions that are deeper than tempo alone. For the purposes of this inquiry, it will be helpful to divide the Gospel phenomenon into two other major kinds (both of which have fast and slow tempo). The Gospel music that was born with Thomas A. Dorsey as its chief architect is considered, for this study, *Historic Gospel*. It is the music of the Great Depression that details clearly and poetically what the religious mood of Black America was all about. That music was penned by Dorsey, Kenneth Morris, Theodore Frye, Doris Akers, Roberta Martin, Lucie Campbell, J. H. Brewster, Sr., and others. This brand of Gospel begins with Dorsey's first composition, "If I Don't Get There," in 1921 and spans the next four decades. *Modern Gospel* is a fairly recent phenomenon; it begins with the tail end of the quartet era in the fifties and the radical social change that developed in the early sixties. Its presence

FIGURE 10

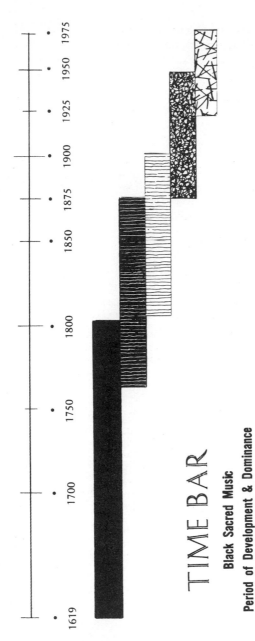

TIME BAR

Black Sacred Music
Period of Development & Dominance

SLAVES UTTERANCES/Moans, Chants, Cries for Deliverance

SPIRITUALS/Faith–Songs, Sorrow Songs, Plantation Hymns, etc.

METER MUSIC/Watts, Wesley, Sankey et al.

HYMNS OF IMPROVISATION/Euro–American hymns with "beat"

GOSPEL MUSIC/Music of Hard Times (Cross fertilization with secular)

and form are still evolving. Modern Gospel, as we shall see later, reflects the influences of both the quartet era and the period symbolized by Martin Luther King's leadership. The distinctions are easily observable and closely tied to the social context of the Black community in America. The appearance of Modern Gospel did not in any way mark the demise of Historic Gospel. Both are very much in evidence, and they exist in parallel fashion with little or no problem. In fact, Historic Gospel, measured by its use and popularity, is stronger than it has ever been.

Some further word might be said here, in introductory fashion, as to the roots of Gospel. Unquestionably the ultimate rootage is in the Spiritual and the earlier musical idioms of Mother Africa. The immediate antecedents came from two directions and two disparate quarters of American life. Thomas A. Dorsey was born in 1899 in Villa Rica, Georgia, thirty-eight miles west of Atlanta.[6] He was the son of a Baptist preacher, and he spent his early years naturally in church services, playing the piano and the "pump" organ. The senior Dorsey was not hostile to blues and jazz, and his son's musical genius was cultivated in both the sacred and secular worlds of music. As a young man, he played with the legendary Tampa Red and accompanied and arranged for both Ma Rainey and Bessie Smith. His proficiency as a pianist and arranger gained for him no small reputation, and he became known widely around the blues circuit as "Georgia Tom" and "Barrelhouse Tom."[7]

The religious influences of Dorsey's early life were persistent, and after a serious illness he devoted his life to religious compositions, beginning with "If I Don't Get There" in 1921. Dorsey admits today that he was especially influenced in his style of religious compositions by Charles Albert Tindley, pastor of Tindley Temple in Philadelphia, Pennsylvania, a (United) Methodist preacher and author of "Stand by Me," "Beams of Heaven," "I'll Overcome," and "We'll Understand It Better, By and By." Gospel music was born of Dorsey's early religious life and the Tindley influence, combined with his experience in the blues-jazz world. In its simplest form Gospel music became a social comment within a religious context, and its musical vehicle was the beat and syncopation of what was known as "worldly" music, coupled with the spontaneity common to all Black music. Dorsey combined the attractive musical forms of the secular world with the sincerity and religiosity of C. A. Tindley. The combination struck at the very heart of the Black religious experience. Boyer comments on Dorsey's genius:

> Prof. Dorsey was the first musician to organize and sophisticate the "call and response" technique of textual treatment in Afro-American songs which had been brought to this country by the slaves and impressed upon Black American culture through its use in the songs of holiness and fundamental Black congregations.[8]

Close scrutiny of the historical development of what is termed "secular" music will reveal that Dorsey's combination of musical talent and experience was absolutely honest, for the separate ingredients which produced "Gospel" have precisely the same root. The same pattern obtains in the matter of the Modern Gospel phenomenon. If there is a variance, it is that the secular world probably gained more in the exchange. The use of "updated" Spirituals by the nonviolent movement created a broad acceptance of religious music with a message via television coverage and instantaneous news reporting. That circumstance, coupled with the influence of the quartet era on the entertainment world, plowed most of the ground in which Modern Gospel was to grow. A quick review of the religious quartets, in dress and style and routine, immediately discloses where such famous pop groups as the Supremes, the Temptations, and the Four Tops found their style. The parallel rise of rhythm and blues and its similarity to the "Gospel" beat have made the influence of the two arenas very much like a two-way street. The world of Gospel has had a profound impact on show business, and the show business world has unalterably affected what is now taking place in the Gospel world *and* institutionalized religious life.

As C. A. Tindley broke the ground for the Historic Gospel music symbolized by Thomas A. Dorsey, the freedom movement in the South was the precursor of the broadly accepted Modern or Pop Gospel of the present.

The Period of Gospel Music

In the discussion and analysis of Gospel music, there are two historical periods associated with the kind of Gospel being reviewed. Quite naturally, there is some overlapping, but the division will help order the exposition. The period of Historic Gospel is 1930–1960, and the period of Modern Gospel is 1960 to the present.

The Great Depression—1925–1940

Crises in the nation affect the poor earlier, and the effects are of longer duration. The economic disaster of 1929 was no exception. Most Blacks in this republic were poor, and the Depression began with them in the mid-twenties, lasting until defense contracts were let for World War II. The fading vitality of the Harlem Renaissance was a symbolic last gasp of Black America's hopes and dreams to be a part of the American mainstream, just before the crash of the stock market in 1929.

The Harlem Renaissance that was born in the post–World War I era was significant politically as well as culturally. One of the sobering effects of the "Great War" on America was the developing of broad interest of American writers in the republic's social and economic problems. Sinclair Lewis and Theodore Dreiser led the way in laying bare the veneer-covered problems of the young nation.[9] It took only a few years for novelists, dramatists, and poets to discover the "Negro problem." There followed a profusion of writing about the Negro which was so powerful that White America began to listen. The Black man in America (at least in the artistic world) used his cultural gifts as a vehicle for ventilating and exposing the many social sins of the larger group.

The leaders of that period still loom large in Black letters. A Jamaican, Claude McKay, was considered by most critics the first significant writer of the Harlem Renaissance. He was followed by the marvelously gifted Countee Cullen, Jean Toomer, Langston Hughes, and James Weldon Johnson. Black musicals and plays were hits on Broadway. The spirit of the Renaissance briefly spread across the entire nation, but Harlem remained its spiritual center. It was during the heyday of the Renaissance that Marcus Garvey strode the stage of Harlem, waving the magic wand of his "Back to Africa" movement, which collapsed with his deportation to Jamaica in 1927. The years preceding the stock market crash were culturally perhaps the richest and most prolific during the odyssey of the Black people in America. Then—Black Friday!

The prelude in Black life to the nation's economic disaster was characterized by deeply entrenched cynicism and despair. The mood of pessimism had come as a result of the terrible riots after World War I and the continuing hypocrisy of the nation in the treatment of its Black citizens. Lerone Bennett asserts that the prevailing mood did much to make the Garvey movement possible.[10] It is an understatement to say that Black folk were unprepared for the Depression years. Democracy eluded them at every turn, and, with the rest of the national community, the Depression swallowed what shreds remained of the American Dream.

It is difficult to fathom how Black folk survived the Depression, so far-reaching and devastating were its effects throughout American life. Lester Granger, the venerable National League executive, is reported to have said that Negro America "almost fell apart."[11]

Black banks and businesses failed like all others. There was little exemption in the throes of Depression. The period was, ironically, a democratization of pain, though the shares were never equal. The slide in Black folks' fortunes remained unchecked until the next war.

Even in tragedy, the Black community demonstrated remarkable resiliency. The Black Church enterprise, though affected by the trauma of the Depression, managed to survive and grow. It continued as the preeminent force in the affairs of the Black community, and in crisis it provided internal stability.[12] "Sweet Jesus" saw many Blacks through the Depression. Paradoxically, some political gains were made during the days of the nation's economic disaster. The population shifts of Blacks to urban centers in the North created a new set of political relationships which Blacks began to make useful. In 1900, nine out of ten Blacks lived in the rural areas; by the mid-thirties, millions populated the concrete ghettos in the North's industrial centers.[13] In 1928, Oscar DePriest was elected to Congress.[14] During Hoover's administration, John H. Parker, a white racist, was nominated for the Supreme Court but defeated by Negro political pressure. In 1936, thousands of Negroes defected from the party of Lincoln to the candidacy of Franklin Delano Roosevelt.[15] Black political power, even in the midst of economic chaos, was making its presence felt.

World War II and the Postwar Era—1940–1954

Despite the second-class status of Blacks in America, they kept abreast of what was going on in the rest of the world, especially as the events related to darker-skinned people and the oppressed. The rise of fascism in Europe was accompanied by the Black community's hatred of Nazism and rejection of its doctrine of Aryan supremacy.[16] The invasion of Poland in early September, 1939, brought the United States a giant step away from its position of neutrality. The fall of Denmark, Norway, the Netherlands, Luxembourg, and Belgium in the spring of 1940 moved the nation closer to the vortex of World War II. Pearl Harbor settled the question of America's involvement, and the struggle for the preservation of the Four Freedoms was joined.

As far as Black people were concerned, World War II was a rerun of World War I. Their participation in the military and the defense effort was accepted hesitantly at first, in normal segregated fashion. By wartime peak, more than a million members of the Black population, male and female, were in uniform, and by late 1944 nearly one-half million were in foreign theaters of war. Black fighting men fought in segregated units, but World War II marked their initial combat service in the Navy, Marines, and Air Corps. As in the first War, Blacks distinguished themselves, especially in the European theater of operations. Outbreaks of racial violence erupted at home and abroad, in the military and among civilians. Even in national crises, the specter of race conflict was always close at hand.

During the mobilization for the war effort, A. Philip Randolph, in a showdown of political strategy with President Roosevelt, forced the issuing of Executive Order 8802, banning discrimination in war industries and the armed services. Randolph called off a proposed March on Washington by 100,000 on the day the order was issued— June 25, 1941.[17] The leverage of Black political clout was firmly established.

Once again, a world war had provided the opportunity for Blacks to be employed in industries and jobs from which they had been systematically excluded. Though the Great Depression had slowed the drive for education, it was not stopped. The combination of college-trained professionals and the increased employment in industry during the war years produced a significant number of middle-class Blacks who were able to articulate and finance the rising expectancy of the Black community.

Part and parcel of that struggle was the work of the NAACP. Under the brilliant leadership of Charles Houston, Thurgood Marshall, William Hastie, and others, the persistent legal forays of the NAACP began to crack the once-invulnerable wall of segregation.[18] The Negro press played a pivotal role in this struggle, sensationalizing racial injustices at home and abroad. So spirited was the journalistic attack during the days of the war that Lerone Bennett reports that the federal government considered "suggestions that Negro publishers be prosecuted for impeding the war effort."[19] It was this climate of skepticism, bitterness, and dissatisfaction that Randolph fused into his successful ploy to secure Executive Order 8802. In the closing days of the war, the NAACP determined that the gains made in race relations during a time of national crisis should be solidified. The decision was made that an all-out attack be made on segregation. The starting foil was segregation in graduate school cases in Texas and Oklahoma. Separate but equal was dealt a final deathblow in the now famous *Brown* v. *Board of Education* decision which the Supreme Court handed down unanimously in 1954.[20] The *Brown* decision was of historic proportions, for it removed for the first time the legal superstructure that kept segregation intact either by legal fiat or by custom and mores. The relentless activity of the Black community, chiefly through the NAACP, had made a major breakthrough in Black-White relations, possibly the most important since the Emancipation Proclamation.

The role of Harry Truman, successor to Franklin Delano Roosevelt, must not be overlooked in the arena of civil rights. His Missouri background evoked some trepidation among Blacks, and Roosevelt's loss was keenly felt because of his and his wife's role in giving attention to the plight of Negroes during the Depression. However, the haberdasher from Missouri proved to be resourceful and forthright in the matter of Black-White relations. In 1948, he issued an executive order requiring fair employment in federal service, declaring that "the principles on which our Government is based require a policy of fair employment throughout the Federal establishment without discrimination because of race, color, religion, or national origin. . . ."[21] Without a lot of fanfare, Truman desegregated the armed services during the Korean War. The full participation in a Second World War within a generation and the measurable gains of the postwar era seemed to augur well the hopes and aspirations of Black people in America. The Supreme Court decision of 1954 appeared to be the gateway to full equality—*at last!*

Martin Luther King, Jr., to Richard Nixon—1955–1968

The elimination of segregation in public education seemed to many the long-awaited promise so often deferred. Of course, the promise's fulfillment would not be tomorrow, but it would be soon! The highest tribunal in the land had spoken, but the Southern reaction was swift and vitriolic. Within two months, the White Citizens Council was formed in Indianola, Mississippi, and the movement spread across the Deep South. Bennett includes a reference to them as "white-collar Ku Klux Klans."[22] A Yale-educated Mississippi jurist, Tom Brady, wrote a book entitled *Black Monday,* describing the Court's decision as a plot to foster miscegenation. Brady, the intellectual leader of the resistance that was to follow, pledged, "We have, through our forefathers, died before for our sacred principles. We can, if necessary, die again."[23] The legislatures of the South rang with cries of "Interposition" and "Nullification." There was even some talk of "Secession" and "States Rights," and the rallying cry of the South became "Never." It is difficult to say finally whether the fierce reaction in the South cowed the Court. It is a matter of record that a year passed before any further action was suggested. One entire year passed, and the Court obtusely ordered public school desegregation, with the innocuous phrase "with all deliberate speed."

Into the vacuum created by the Court's weak-kneed posture on its own unanimous decree came Martin Luther King, Jr. A Depression event (his birth on January 15, 1929) began to take on worldwide significance in the unlikeliest of places—Montgomery, Alabama. Lerone Bennett's narrative is classic: "Martin Luther King, Jr., moved the struggle from the courtroom to the streets, from law libraries to the pews of the churches, from the mind to the soul."[24]

The Montgomery bus protest captured the fancy and support of the nation and much of the world. What had begun as a demonstration for a better form of segregation (first-come-first-serve basis) developed under King's skillful and charismatic leadership into a holy cause. What was aimed at a week's duration stretched into 385 days of "tired feet and rested souls." Jim Crow was very much alive in the Deep South, but major surgery was performed at Montgomery. At the end of the bus boycott, almost all of Black America had been involved in one way or another. The period ushered in by the Montgomery bus protest is of enormous significance. There is very little question that Montgomery opened the door to a period of the most frenetic activity in the history of race relations in America. It can be best described in terms of its growth, development, and significance by what the author has termed the Concentric Circle Development of the nonviolent movement in America. The accompanying chart in Figure 11 details the progressive development.

The Supreme Court decision of 1954 held promise in the Black psyche of righting the wrongs that had been so everlasting. The Court's inability or lack of will transmitted the hoax to the heart of Black America. Martin Luther King, Jr., a Black Brahmin of well-to-do parentage, credentialed by Boston University, young, gifted, and a Black preacher, introduced the modern techniques of Gandhi, wrapped up in the religion and morality of the folk churches. King's nonviolent program of attack against an old enemy (segregation) on a scale of mass involvement constructively channeled the bitter and frustrated energies of a people too often betrayed. The sociohistorical analysis follows (analysis is keyed to chart in Figure 11).

1. *Montgomery, Alabama* (1955–1956). The significance of the Montgomery bus protest is that it represents the initial instance of the nonviolent method being utilized in race relations *on a mass scale.* A traditional form of segregation (intracity bus transportation) was engaged, and the ensuing protest was so powerful that a climate of acceptance was established by the time the issue was finally settled by court decree.

2. *Sit-In Movement* (1960). In contradistinction to Montgomery, which was local and legally resolved, the central issue of the Sit-In Movement was service at food counters in chain and variety stores. The focus was regional (Southwide, with sympathy demonstrations in the North), and the resolution hinged on the boycott methodology, which prompted negotiation and conciliation.

3. *Freedom Ride* (1961). The Freedom Ride, initiated by the Congress of Racial Equality, sustained by the Southern Christian Leadership Conference, and fueled by students, was national in scope

FIGURE 11

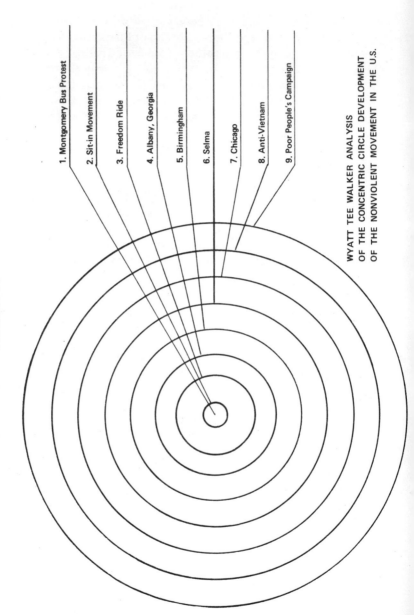

1. Montgomery Bus Protest
2. Sit-in Movement
3. Freedom Ride
4. Albany, Georgia
5. Birmingham
6. Selma
7. Chicago
8. Anti-Vietnam
9. Poor People's Campaign

WYATT TEE WALKER ANALYSIS
OF THE CONCENTRIC CIRCLE DEVELOPMENT
OF THE NONVIOLENT MOVEMENT IN THE U.S.

since the focus of the attack—interstate travel—involved the machinery of the Department of Justice and the Interstate Commerce Commission. The mobilized national sentiment focused on Jackson, Mississippi, and New Orleans, Louisiana, and forced resolution of the problem via an order from the Interstate Commerce Commission (a nonlegislative resolution).

4. *Albany, Georgia* (1961–1962). By this time, the nonviolent movement was picking up experience, momentum, and support. Southern legislatures began to pass specious laws aimed at draining away the enthusiasm of picketing and marching. In response, the movement took up the cry, "We'll fill the jails." Albany was the first instance of the literal fulfillment of that slogan. Not only were the city and county jails filled to capacity on two occasions, but surrounding county jails were filled as well. A strategic error was made in the Albany campaigns. The movement had too many targets, and the strength of the community was diluted, with a veritable stalemate resulting. It should be noted that though no integration took place, the local bus company was put out of business (boycott) and the library was closed, as were the bus terminal, lunch counters, public schools, and recreational facilities. The significance of Albany is that the movement forces learned how to mobilize an entire community for an attack on segregation.

5. *Birmingham, Alabama* (1963). The lesson of the Albany campaign was clear. The movement narrowed its attack on the commerce and industry of the South's largest city and worst city in terms of race relations. The mobilization was begun nearly a year in advance. Hardly any sage will deny that the Birmingham confrontation was one of the chief watersheds of the nonviolent movement. The 1964 Civil Rights Act was an immediate and direct result, in addition to the movement having gained legitimacy and national strength. The March on Washington followed that same summer with 250,000 in attendance.

6. *Selma to Montgomery* (1965). Despite the outlawing of the grandfather clause and the abolition of the White primary, the right of the franchise for Blacks in the Deep South was, at best, theoretical. The Selma campaign, bloody and costly, climaxed with a march to the state's capital that influenced the passage of the Voting Rights Act of 1965. Black sheriffs, mayors, legislators, and other public officials

are now frequently found in many areas throughout the Deep South.

7. *Chicago* (1966). With desegregation of public facilities in the South a reality, the problems of the South were now seen to be the problems of the urban centers. *De facto* segregation in public schools, a raging Northern as well as Southern issue, remained entrenched because of housing segregation. The King forces reasoned that nonviolence should be tried in the North. King admitted he faced the bitterest resistance of his career in this campaign. The nonviolent movement left Chicago with an "E" for effort and an open housing covenant that has since proved unenforceable.

8. *Anti-Vietnam* (1967). The addition of King's voice to the peace movement splintered the broad support that his movement had gained. The cost was high: liberal Whites, fair-weather Jews, bourgeois Blacks, Roy Wilkins, Whitney Young, the White House (Carl Rowan did the dirty work),[25] and scared preachers, Black and White, fell by the wayside. King, now a Nobel laureate, stuck to his convictions. One year, to the day, after his major (April 4, 1967) speech against the war in Southeast Asia, he was the victim of an assassin's bullet in Memphis, Tennessee. He had interrupted his plans for the Poor People's Campaign to join the garbage workers in that Southern city in their effort for collective bargaining.

9. *Poor People's Campaign* (1968). The morality of the Black people's struggle in America was verified by their gains. Every time Black folks made a stride forward, others benefited as well. Thus, the Negro's drive for integration raised the issue of quality education for all. The Poor People's Campaign represented the broadest base of the nonviolent movement in America. While King's successor, Ralph Abernathy, was galvanizing America on behalf of the Black poor primarily, the nation discovered the American Indian, the Hispanics of the industrial centers, the Chicanos of the Southwest, and the Appalachian Whites. Despite the (posthumous) detractors of King's stand, the sociological importance of that coalition cannot be minimized. The race/class struggle will move forward only with the strength of that same coalition.

The foregoing analysis provides a broad sweep of the period in question and underscores an irony of fact. The King era did involve *more* humanity, more ergs of energy, untold thousands of dollars, countless court briefs and litigation, and some precious lives and limbs. But with all the gains visible and invisible, the changes have been more symbolic than substantive. Twenty years after the Supreme Court decision struck down segregation in public education, antibusing riots raged in Boston. The forces in White America that always resisted full equality for Black folks had regrouped, and the adversary was more formidable than ever. It was no wonder—in fact, it was probable and predictable—that a Richard Nixon would rise to power after a period that was so promising and hopeful in the affairs of the Black community.

The comparative chart, Figure 12, reveals an alarming similarity in the flow of history in the nineteenth and twentieth centuries. Immediately following Reconstruction, after Blacks had made identifiable gains, the wheels of progress were shifted into reverse, and the century ended with *Plessy* v. *Ferguson*—segregation by race with the sanction of the Supreme Court. In the twentieth century, following a period of identifiable gains (the King era), those same wheels had been shifted into reverse, and with the ascendancy of Richard Nixon to the White House, it became apparent that Black folks were worse off then as a group than they were before the Supreme Court's decision of 1954.

The return of Nixon to office in 1972 with the greatest plurality in the history of elective politics sent a message that was loud and clear to Blacks—America has no genuine concern for the Black community.

At this writing, Nixon is gone—driven from public office, largely by his own hand. His demise is symbolic of the only hope and faith Black people have, that "God's gonna destroy this wicked race and raise up a nation that will obey." The Black folk religion, Africanized Christianity, lives and works for its adherents through the continued, persistent reinforcement of its existentialist faith through Black song.

Social Significance of Gospel

The dilemma of the Black people in America has been philosophical as well as practical. For more than three hundred years, they have undergone a process that John Hope Franklin terms *"Americanization."*[26] While that process influenced them in varying degrees, they were forced to live in a separate social and emotional world of their own making. Simultaneously, they became increasingly involved in

FIGURE 12

COMPARATIVE FLOW OF HISTORY IN THE U.S.—19th and 20th CENTURIES
(IN RELATIONSHIP TO THE BLACK CONDITION)

1. SEGREGATION Pattern of segregation engulfed nation either by statute or custom.	**1. SLAVERY** Chattel slavery obtained from 1619 to 1861. Considered by many historians as worst form of human bondage in Western history.
2. 1954 SUPREME COURT DECISION *Brown v. Board of Education*, a landmark decision, overturned *Plessy v. Ferguson* and removed legal buttressing that kept segregation intact.	**2. EMANCIPATION** Executive order of Lincoln freed 4.8 million slaves. Passage of 13th, 14th, 15th Amendments followed.
3. KING ERA Black freedom movement symbolized and led largely by MLK generated two major civil rights bills and 1.5 million new voters in Deep South, while breaking significant new ground.	**3. RECONSTRUCTION** Freedmen, despite handicaps, began ambitious participation in political process, finding representation at local, state, and federal levels.
4. RISE OF NIXON Wheels of Black progress slowed; urban unrest and riots met by white backlash. Assassination of Malcolm X, King, and Robert Kennedy marked period in which *de facto* school segregation in North became more recalcitrant.	**4. POST-RECONSTRUCTION** Marked by Rutherford Hayes's ascendancy to presidency and subsequent withdrawal of troops from South. This action flagged compromise on Negro's political equality.
5. ? ? ? ? ? ? ? Difficult at this moment to guess what new form of white oppression will be attempted.	**5. PLESSY V. FERGUSON** Following a period when rights and gains of Blacks were nullified by legislative, judicial, and executive branches of government at state and federal levels, segregation imposed with sanction of Supreme Court.

the affairs of the dominant society that helped to shape and mold the institutions and life-style that kept their humanity and sanity intact.[27] The Black people were inevitably impaled on the dilemma, practically and philosophically, of trying to live in two worlds at once. This is the same double-consciousness of which W. E. B. Du Bois spoke.[28] The rub has been that the more Americanized they became, the more detrimental it seemed to their psychic well-being. The balance between the two worlds was stabilized by a comfortable sense of identity that is not swallowed by the Americanization. Black folk religion and its music helped to reduce the tension and anxiety of living in those two competing worlds. In the face of repeated broken faith, undisguised oppression, and rampant injustice, the Black community has always returned, musically and otherwise, to the religion of its forebears.

It is no surprise, then, that the Great Depression saw an "in-turning" on the part of Black folks in the face of the economic ravages of the period. One of the clearest evidences of that in-turning was the musical literature coined in the throes of the Depression's dark night. The Gospel era began in the Depression and lasted until the present; it is, then, not only the social comment of hard times, but it is also the testimony of triumphant faith.

The rigor of the Great Depression was only one of several factors that influenced the development of Gospel music. It was born of hard times, but the respite of World War II gave promise of a "new day." A major population shift, similar to that of a generation earlier and another world war, brought Blacks into the industrial North in literal droves. The new opportunities heightened expectancies that were fueled by the gains of the war era and solidified in the postwar period. "God is able" was more than a spirited musical number; it was the witness of the faithful. The rainbow of the Supreme Court decision and the heroics of the nonviolent movement persuaded "the Lord's despised few" that help from heaven was on the way. In summary, the Great Depression, the great migration incident to World War II, the Supreme Court decision, and the subsequent glory days of the King era greatly influenced the shape and development of the Gospel era.

The form and structure of folk music are very often a clear social comment on the specific social context out of which it is born. This is true of the Negro Spiritual and no less true of Gospel music.

> The rise of gospel music around 1930 is attributable to several sociological changes within the black community, foremost among which was the steady increase in migration from the south by blacks in search of greater economic opportunities and freedom. With these migrants came their religious traditions which found an outlet for expression in the various humble store fronts and small church buildings which some congregations could afford. . . . The musical traditions of these various denominations were maintained in the more fundamentalist-type churches, providing the greatest opportunity for the seeds of gospel music to come into full bloom.[29]

The creation of Gospel music is a social statement that, in the face of America's rejection and economic privation, Black folks made a conscious decision to be themselves. It was an early stage of identity awakening and identity nourishing. It signaled a return to "roots." The basis of Gospel repertoire is the "Dr. Watts" style hymn that carries all the nostalgia of early childhood, the "mourner's bench," and religious conversion during the twilight years when one was no longer a child and not yet an adult. The "Dr. Watts" themes invariably extol indomitable faith in the face of desperate circumstances (see meter music, chapter 5).

It is of some significance that during the early development of Gospel, this new music was often met with some hostility on the pretext, sometimes sincere, that it was "sin music." Thomas A. Dorsey, the Father of Gospel, confesses that this early rejection fired his determination to "carry the banner." The lukewarm reception to "Gospel" in the established churches reminds one of Bishop Payne's excoriation of the Spiritual and jubilee music nearly one hundred years earlier.[30] Both reflect an attitude of nonacceptance of self on the part of the hesitant.

Dorsey persevered; he went to the churches that received him and frequented the National Baptist Convention until the new music caught on. As the Depression receded, Gospel became more popular and acceptable. Pearl Williams-Jones notes the reason:

> There was, and has been, an unquenchable thirst among these people for their own music which could express their innermost feelings about God, and their emotional involvement which was a part of this expression. The music at hand was an idiom with which they were all familiar and it could be created spontaneously. The preacher, the song leader, and congregation all shared equally in those creative moments.[31]

One spinoff of the reticence of "main line" churches to accept Gospel was that the music quickly created its own world, and into the forties it existed, in part, as a quasi-underground church, filling auditoriums and arenas with Gospel concerts. The crisis of World War II brought a lot of the brothers and sisters "home" to the Gospel idiom. In the postwar era, Gospel enjoyed its golden era and marked the transfer of the Gospel sound to the entertainment world.

Thematically, Gospel speaks of life just as it is. Heilbut in his remarkable book speaks eloquently of this basic characteristic:

> Gospel lyrics may sound banal, but they talk about the things that matter most to poor people. When you're well off, you can write songs about individual neuroses. But a poor man's concerns are . . . staying alive ("I could have been dead sleeping in my grave"; "It's another day's journey and I'm glad about it"); healthy ("I've been sick and I couldn't get well"; "I woke up this morning in sound mind . . . with the blood running *warm* in my veins"); and financially solvent ("I've been down and out, you know I didn't have a dime"; "When your meal gets down low and you have no place to go"). Combine these pressing demands with a diction made up of the most vivid idioms and some of the most old-fashioned imagery, and the gospel language begins to make sense.[32]

The revival of interest in the Spiritual during both World War II and the King era served to strengthen Gospel. The Gospel world quickly took note of what was going on in the South and saw their idiom as an instrument in the struggle for freedom and dignity. Mahalia Jackson, Cleophus Robinson, Clara Ward, and others raised thousands of dollars by their singing for the freedom struggle in the South. Robinson, a Baptist preacher as well as a giant in the Gospel field, declared, "We're gonna keep on singing our song and make Big Brother give us our due!"

The psychic healthiness of self-expression within the Black cultural context is a sufficient salutary aspect of the Gospel phenomenon itself. Add to that the faith substance that marshals the human spirit in the most trying of circumstances and the down-to-earth, plain-spoken idiom which disarms completely, and Gospel is revealed as one of the world's great Black arts.

Profile of Gospel: Historic and Modern

It is no small task to give a profile of Gospel in such limited space. The task looms larger when one considers the great musical and

FIGURE 13
BLACK SACRED MUSIC
Diagram of "Blood Line"*

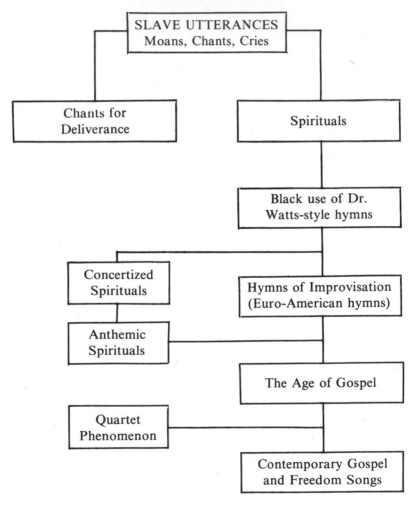

*Adapted from Wendel Whalum's diagram appearing in *Review and Expositor,* Spring, 1972, p. 581.

artistic breadth Gospel covers. Tony Heilbut, an accepted authority on Gospel, speaks to this fact:

... gospel has as much variety as any popular musical form extant. We're all familiar with the great-voiced soloists symbolized by Mahalia Jackson. Likewise "O Happy Day" by the Edwin Hawkins Singers introduced to the world the fiery, adventurous harmonies of the young peoples' choirs. But there's so much else. Gospel influences, reflects and mimics blues, jazz, and even country and western. There are male quartets who sound like the Golden Gate Quartet, the jubilee group with the impressive close harmonies that first turned America on to swinging pop-gospel versions of the spirituals we learn in public school. Then there are male groups who can and do teach James Brown and Wilson Pickett lessons in frenzy. There are the Edwin Hawkins Singers and dozens of new choirs into jazz chord progressions and Mormon Tabernacle decibels. ... Roebuck Staple's guitar sounds like simple blues. ... In Chicago they call the pianist Geraldine Gay "the Errol Garner of gospel," and in Philadelphia, Pearl Williams Jones is cited as "our Nina Simone."[33]

The reader will note that the profile of Gospel is heavily laden with name references. One of the characteristics of the Gospel arena is that it is personality oriented. Heilbut says, "It's the singer, not the song," to note the reverse emphasis. The Gospel world is best traced through its exponents and their experiences, hardships, and tribulations. Tony Heilbut has done an extensive and in-depth study in the book *The Gospel Sound,* referred to above. It provides a deep sense of the feel and touch of the world of Gospel and its devotees, revealing many subtle insights about which the general lay public is completely unaware. It is a book of considerable import in the field of music, secular or sacred.

The reader is aware that the roots of Gospel are in the Spiritual. In much the same way that the original Spirituals were altered, influenced by the specific social context, and transmitted by word of mouth (oral tradition), the Gospel idiom has developed. It is impossible to fix precise dates, but it is safe to say that following the pre-Gospel era, three distinct phases of Gospel movement are observable. The first phase begins with Thomas Dorsey and his small cadre of troops who doggedly persisted in introducing the "new music" to Black America. A second phase is discernible after Dorsey, Roberta Martin, and Theodore Frye. Kenneth Morris, Lillian Bowles, and Sallie Martin had established the "gospel circuit," with traveling choirs, trios, duos, and sheet music. This phase has been termed the "golden age of Gospel" with the big names touring the country and filling arenas with its committed adherents and local talent. This second phase was also the period of the quartet phenomenon mentioned earlier. The third phase parallels the freedom movement in the South and displays the broadest exchange of influences between the "sacred" and "secular" world of Black music. It might prove helpful to look at Gospel—the music and the personnel—with a view toward appreciating more clearly the distinct phenomenon of Black sacred music.

The Pre-Gospel Era—1905–1925

Just as religious music was altered in its development and reflective of the social context of the people who made use of it, the same forces were at work in the secular world. Wendel Whalum notes this parallel:

> The first three decades of the century also saw the shift, in the world of secular music, from ragtime to blues, to the recording of the blues, and the introduction of jazz. In no small measure did these expressions have their effect on gospel music. In fact, one of the leaders in the gospel music movement, Thomas A. Dorsey (b. 1899), was active as a blues pianist and, before 1919, had been one of the successful pianists in the south . . .[34]

It was in this same era that Charles Albert Tindley and Lucie Campbell began to publish a type of hymn-form Gospel that gained wide popularity in the Black religious community. Tindley was Dorsey's greatest influence in lyric style. The "soul-stirring" songs of this era were issued in the publications of the National Baptist Convention. *Gospel Pearls* and *The Baptist Standard Hymnal* remain extant today. A sample of two standards of this era appear below: "Some Day" by Tindley and "He'll Understand and Say, 'Well Done'" by Campbell. The music, notations, and lyrics of another sample of this era are found at the end of this chapter.

Some Day

Beams of Heaven as I go
Through this wilderness below
Guide my feet in peaceful ways,
Turn my midnight into days.

When in the darkness I would grope,
Faith always sees a star of hope,
And soon from all life's grief and danger
I shall be free some day.

Chorus

I do not know how long it will be,
Nor what the future holds for me
But this I know, if Jesus leads me,
I shall be free some day.[35]

He'll Understand and Say, "Well Done"

If when you give the best of your service
Telling the world that the Savior has come,
Be not dismayed when men don't believe you;
He'll understand, He'll say, "Well done."

Chorus

Oh, when I come to the end of my journey,
Weary of life, the battle is won,
Carrying the staff and cross of redemption
He'll understand, He'll say, "Well done."[36]

The Dorsey Era—1930–1945

Thomas Dorsey is the epitome of Gospel music. He and Sallie
Martin organized the National Convention of Gospel Choirs and
Choruses in 1932, the first Black Gospel music convention. A year
earlier, he and another colleague, Theodore Frye, organized the first
Gospel choir in the Ebenezer Baptist Church in Chicago. After a
serious illness in the mid-twenties, this former blues pianist and
arranger turned to composing and arranging religious music
exclusively. In the same year that he organized the Convention, he
opened the Dorsey House of Music.[37] It was Dorsey who introduced
Mahalia Jackson to Chicago audiences and for several years traveled
with her as composer-arranger. Hardly anyone of this period in the
Gospel field remained untouched by the genius of Tom Dorsey. The
names of the era are legendary: Sallie and Roberta Martin, Theodore
Frye, Kenneth Morris, Lillian Bowles, Mahalia Jackson, J. Herbert
Brewster, Sr., and the youngster of the pioneers, Clara Ward. As the
Gospel circuit grew, the music of these religious troubadours found

broader acceptance in the churches across America that had once frowned on the "beat" of Gospel. As America moved toward World War II, Gospel music had become an entrenched part of the Black religious experience. Three samples of this era follow:

If You See My Savior

I was standing by the bedside of a neighbor,
Who was just about to cross the swelling tide,
And I asked him if he would do me a favor:
Kindly take this message to the other side.

Chorus

If you see my Savior, tell Him that you saw me,
When you saw me, I was on my way,
You may meet some old friend who may ask for me,
Tell them I am coming home some day.[38]

Lord, I've Tried

I have never reached perfection, but I've tried;
Sometimes I have lost connection, but I've tried;
Sometimes right and sometimes wrong,
Hoping some day to be strong,
Then I'll rise and sing this song—Lord, I've tried.

Chorus

Lord, I've tried (Lord, I've tried),
Lord, I've tried (Lord, I've tried),
Yes, I've tried (Yes, I've tried),
I've really tried (really tried)
To be (be just what you'd)
Just what you'd have (have me to be),
Me to be (be just what you'd have me to be);
Sometimes up (sometimes up) and
Sometimes down (sometimes down),
Almost level (almost level)
To the ground (to the ground),
Still I'm climbing (still I'm climbing)
Round by round (round by round).
Lord, I've tried (Lord, I've really tried).[39]

Didn't It Rain

It rained forty days and it rained forty nights,
there wasn't no land nowhere in sight;

God sent a raven to bring the news, he hoist
his wings and away he flew;
To the East (listen to the rain), to the West
(listen to the rain), to the North (listen to
the rain), to the South (listen to the rain).
All day (listen to the rain), all night (listen
to the rain), tell me (listen to it).

Chorus

Didn't it rain, children (children, didn't it)
rain;
Oh, my Lord (didn't it), oh (didn't it),
oh (didn't it);
Oh, my Lord, didn't it rain.[40]
(Repeat.)

Gospel's Golden Era—1945–1960

So large did the influence of Dorsey loom over the world of Gospel
that during the forties and fifties most Gospel music was referred to as
"Dorsey's." This period of Gospel felt the influence of the wartime
Wings over Jordan choir and several jubilee quartets: Southernaires,
the Golden Gate, the Charioteers, and the Dixie Humming Birds.
The popularity and the broadcasts inspired "more authentic" groups
to enter the broadcast and recording world. The Georgia Peach
appeared at Radio City Music Hall, and Sister Rosetta Tharpe
turned up in a few nightclubs. Heilbut, in referring to this period,
remarks that Gospel "became the most important black musical form
since early jazz."[41]

In the early fifties, some Gospel groups were commanding as much
as four-figure guarantees, and recordings in the field began to
proliferate. Black-oriented radio programs played nearly as much
Gospel as they did rock and roll.

This golden period of Gospel embraced the brightest days of the
quartet phenomenon, the real antecedents of the Drifters and others.
Heilbut alleges that quartet singing antedated the pioneer days of
Dorsey and Sallie Martin. He considers "Gospel groups" a recent
development.[42] Two distinct styles exist within Gospel: quartet is the
older but not the best known; the newer style is simply called "gospel"
and embraces soloists, groups, and choirs.

The world of Gospel ebbed and flowed with its chief currency:

people. Their heritage of an oral tradition gave a sense of community in song. The "Gospel legends" were the lead singers of the quartets— R. H. Harris, Silas Steele, Walter Latimore, Ira Tucker, Archie Brownlcc, Kylo Turner, Sam McCrary, Julius Cheeks. Venerable Gospel singers like J. Robert Bradley, Norsalus McKissick, Raymond Rassbery, Robert Anderson, and Joe May have been "wrecking" churches for a generation. The female singers are the most exciting. Queen C. Anderson, Willie Mae Ford Smith, Sallie Martin, Mahalia Jackson, Ernestine Washington, Rosetta Tharpe, Roberta Martin, Sadie Durham, and Edna Gallmon Cooke were the hallmark singers of the pioneer days. The second generation Gospel queens included Marion Williams, Bessie Griffin, Dorothy Love Coates, Myrtle Scott, Deloris Barrett Campbell, Clara Ward, Ruth Davis, Bessie Folk, Albertina Walker, and Inez Andrews. The plethora of names mirrors the huge field that Gospel represents, with more devotees than any other music form in America.[43] Three samples of this era follow:

Lead Me, Guide Me

Chorus

Lead me, guide me along the way;
Lord, if you lead me, I can't stray.
Lord, let me walk each day with thee,
Lead me, O Lord, lead me, guide me.

I am weak and I need thy strength and power
To help me on my way in the darkest hour,
Let me through the darkness Thy face to see;
Lead me, O Lord, lead me.[44]

God Is Still on the Throne

When in distress, just call Him;
If you're oppressed, just call Him;
When storms assail you and others have failed you,
Yes, God is still on the throne.

Chorus

God is still on the throne
Within your bosom you have the phone
Where'er you walk

You're not walking alone;
Remember, God is still on the throne.[45]

Holding My Savior's Hand

I shall have life everlasting
Holding my Savior's hand;
I shall have joy for the asking
Holding my Savior's hand;
Free from the world and its sorrows,
Free from all doubts and fears,
I shall rejoice forever
Holding my Savior's hand.

Chorus

Holding the Savior's hand,
Viewing the promised land,
Nothing on earth can stop me
From holding my Savior's hand.
　　　(holding His hand).[46]

The Era of Modern Gospel—1960 to the Present

It is difficult to make any conclusions about this phase of the Gospel movement since the vantage point of history is much too brief. Some trends have developed, and the significant influences that have touched Gospel can be pointed out, but beyond that, little can be said conclusively. It is simply too early to tell.

Three distinct trends are apparent and intimately interrelated. The first two are very much like the chicken-and-the-egg dilemma. During the height of the freedom struggle in the South, the nation, Black and White, had *rediscovered the authentic Spiritual*. They were on the lips of the demonstrators of the South, but with very specific word changes that spoke of the immediate social context. See Figure 14. Radio and television transmission conjured up old memories of religious roots long since forgotten. Overnight, it seems that *Freedom Songs were born*. Of course, they were not new, just revamped, and the youngsters and the oldsters of the movement had reclaimed them through an oral tradition of music that bridged the generation gap. The music of the struggle soon belonged to any sympathetic supporter of the movement.

FIGURE 14
The Birth of Freedom Songs*

Refrain

I want Jesus to walk with me,
Yes, I want Jesus to walk with me;
All along my pilgrim journey,
Lord, I want Jesus to walk with me.

I want Jesus to walk with me,
Yes, I want Jesus to walk with me;
All along *this Freedom* journey,
Lord, I want Jesus to walk with me.

Stanza

When I'm in trouble,
Lord, walk with me;
When I'm in trouble,
Lord, walk with me.
All along my pilgrim journey,
Lord, I want Jesus to walk with me.

Down in the jailhouse,
Lord, walk with me
Down in the jailhouse,
Lord, walk with me.
All along *this Freedom* journey,
Lord, I want Jesus to walk with me.

Woke up this mornin' with my mind
    Stayed on Jesus;
Woke up this mornin' with my mind
    Stayed on Jesus;
Woke up this mornin' with my mind
    Stayed on Jesus;
Hal-le-lu, hal-le-lu, hal-le-lu-jah!

Woke up this mornin' with my mind
    Stayed on *Freedom;*
Woke up this mornin' with my mind
    Stayed on *Freedom;*
Woke up this mornin' with my mind
    Stayed on *Freedom;*
Hal-le-lu (hal-le-lu), hal-le-lu
    (hal-le-lu), hal-le-lu-jah!

Oh, Freedom! Oh, Freedom!
Oh, Freedom over me;
And befo'ah I'd be a slave
I'd be buried in my grave
And go home to my Lord and be free.

No more weeping, etc.

No more moaning (mourning), etc.

No more dyin', etc.

(This spiritual hymn's refrain is
sung in its exact original form.)

No more segregation, etc.

No more Jim Crow, etc.

*Wyatt Tee Walker, "The Soulful Journey of the Negro Spiritual," *Negro Digest* July, 1963, p. 93.

Simultaneously, *there began a transfer of the gospel influence to the world of entertainment.* The similarities of rhythm and blues, the superstardom of Aretha Franklin, and the alumni of the quartet and Gospel world's invasion of the pop world all congealed to create in America the so-called "soul" concept. Mahalia Jackson's wry comment is apropos: "After all, we invented it. All this mess you hear calling itself soul ain't nothing but warmed-over gospel." Too much has been said about the influence of jazz and blues on Gospel without enough being written about Gospel's influence on the secular world of entertainment. A little close observation will reveal that the influences have traveled a busy two-way street and most of the traffic is coming from the direction of Black sacred music. Heilbut's comment quoted on page 147 is proof text of that fact. Add to that, style, beat, idiosyncrastic performance, improvisation, and the overwhelming numbers of show business stars and superstars who honed their skills in church choirs and before church audiences. It is evident that the world of entertainment *owes* the Black Church.

The widespread support of the freedom struggle and the music that identified it contributed largely to the diminution of the sharp distinctions between sacred and secular music. A new sense of acceptance and pride greeted Black sacred music's earlier stepchild, Gospel. Thus, the third trend is apparent—that is, not only does Gospel have easy access to Black churches universally, but there is also a growing interest in the use of the Gospel form in the churches of dominant society, particularly the more liturgical churches. Nina Simone opened a concert in the nation's capital with a Gospel version of "I Am Thine, O Lord." Donny Hathaway and Roberta Flack sang Gospel style on wax and tape with the mournful "Come, Ye Disconsolate." For weeks in the late sixties, the Edwin Hawkins Singers' version of "O Happy Day" was number one on the pop charts. An even more significant development has been the creation of Gospel choirs at the old-line Black universities. In years past, the classical repertoire of the Black university choir bowed in deference to the Spiritual in the last section of the choir's concert program. They would not even consider singing Gospel. The Black university Gospel choir movement is augmented by the growing numbers of similar choirs at Harvard (Kuumba Singers), Connecticut State, Oberlin, and other predominantly White universities.

This period in the development of Gospel music has at least one unsung hero. The work of Clinton Utterbach, composer and arranger, a pioneer in his own right, represents one of the most significant developments in Gospel. In the early sixties, the Utterbach Choral Ensemble came to considerable national prominence via television appearances and college concert tours. For several years, Utterbach and his group made annual appearances at Carnegie Hall in New York. This kind of itinerary was a far cry from that of most Gospel groups and distinct from the celebrated Gospel groups and singles who were either headlining their own shows or trying their fortunes in nightclubs.

Utterbach, in a 1974 interview, disclosed that two main ingredients contributed to the success of the Ensemble. First, he had observed closely the format of Gospel programs that packed large city auditoriums and noted that the variety of "acts" attracted a wide cross section of devotees. He reasoned that a single group which approximated the "variety" aspect of the program might well perform before large audiences without the hassle of engaging fifteen or twenty different Gospel aggregations. Thus, he arranged his program to approximate the variety of a Gospel extravaganza—but with a single group of singers, well trained and sensitive to the dramatic and improvised quality of Gospel. The concert would begin with a couple of powerful and familiar standards, then a soloist, a trio, a double quartet, an all-male and/or all-female number with the entire group performance interspersed for balance. As in all show business, secular or sacred, there was always the "big finish."

The other ingredient introduced into the Gospel arena by Utterbach was the calculated use of classical techniques in the performance of Gospel. He was the first Gospel devotee to make use of the discipline and techniques of classical European-style music and wed them to the vitality and spirit of Gospel. Utterbach was to Gospel what Dett was to the Spirituals.

Utterbach is author of more than a hundred compositions that reflect his pioneering style. This style is immediately apparent in performance, whether it is an original composition, an old standard, original field Spiritual, or an updated Gospel hymn from the Dorsey era. First, there is the statement of the basic theme, followed by a second section, or "movement," that is an embellishment of the theme, followed by a second and sometimes a third and a fourth embellishment. The second and third sections or "movements" can be revisited as a special refrain or as the section on which the number "goes out," or ends, depending largely upon the audience response and participation.

The evidence of Utterbach's impact is the increasing number of musicians and composers, trained in the classical discipline, who are plying their talents in the Gospel idiom. Andrae Crouch and Robert Frierson are two. It must be noted that a contributing influence to this return to the music of the folk religion is the narrow opportunities of Blacks in the field of classical music, but the return of these sons of Africa augurs well the future of Black sacred music.

With the distinctions between sacred and secular music receding markedly and the introduction of instrumentation into the worship services of the folk churches, the future appears bright for the Gospel idiom. The portent of trained musicians in the Gospel arena is the development of a body of musical literature that weds freshness and spontaneity of Gospel with the form and discipline of Euro-American musical techniques. The promise of the future for Gospel is a place of permanence and respect in the family of American religious music.

On the pages following are several samples of the lyrics of the Gospel music of the modern era. At the end of this chapter are several musical notations that illustrate all three phases of the Gospel era.

Lord, Help Me to Hold Out

Chorus

Lord, help me to hold out,
Lord, help me to hold out,
Lord, help me to hold out
Until my change comes, comes.

My way may not be easy;
You did not say that it would be.
But if it gets dark,
I can't see my way,
You told me to put my trust in Thee
(that's why I'm asking You)[47]

The Failure Is Not in God

The failure's not in God; it's in me, it's in me.
The failure's not in God; it's in me, it's in me.
I haven't done all that I should,
I have not earned all of His good,
The failure's not in God; it's in me, it's in me.[48]

Be a Fence All Around Me

Chorus

Jesus, be a fence all around me.
I want you to protect me as I travel on my way;
Oh, I know you can and I know you will,
You'll fight my battle if I just keep still,
Oh, Lord, be a fence all around me every day.

This is a prayer, Lord,
    That I pray each and every day;
I ask the Lord to guide my footsteps
    As I travel this narrow way.
Lord, keep your arms around me,
    Jesus, keep me day by day,
Come on, Jesus, and be a fence around me
    every, every, every, every day Oh[49]

I'll Send My Son

I sent them Men of Old,
Prophets and Sages Bold,
Warning them Day and Night
Turn to the Path of Right
But they would not heed my Word . . .

And out of Egypt Land
I brought them with my hand
Still they did not obey
From me did turn away
Wretched and lost, there was no one could save . . .

Redemption would free man's Soul
Cleanse Him and make Him whole.
Mortal would not suffice,
But there's one Sacrifice:
I'll send my son so that all might be Saved.

Chorus

I'll send my son so that all might be saved,
    might be saved;
He must die and must go to the grave,
And on the third day He will rise
And ascend unto the sky.
I'll send my son so that all might be saved.[50]

Dedicated to Rev. Leo Simmons

THE FAILURE IS NOT IN GOD
(IT'S IN ME)

Arr. by
ROBERTA MARTIN

By JESSY DIXON

© Copyright 1964 by Jessie Dixon, Chicago, Ill.

CHORUS

The fail-ure's not in God it's in me it's in me The

fail-ure's not in God it's in me it's in me I come

short so man-y times and e-vil thoughts come in to my mind I know the

fail-ure is not in God it's in me it's in me it's not in

CHOIR   SOLOIST   CHOIR

God it's in me it's not in God it's in me I know the

fail-ure is not in God it's in me it's in me.

DIDN'T IT RAIN
(Spiritual)

W. M. Webb Arrangement

As sung by the famous Martin and Frye Quartet,
Robert Anderson, Soloist

Words and Music by
ROBERTA MARTIN

Lively

Did-n't it rain _____ chil-dren   Rain   oh, my
(chil-dren did- n't it)

LEAD   CHORUS   LEAD   CHORUS   LEAD

Lord, _____   (Did-n't it,)   oh, _____   (Did-n't it,)   oh, _____   (Did - n't it,)

CHORUS   VERSE (Sop. Solo - Chorus *hum*)

oh, My Lord did-n't it rain.
1. It rained for-ty days and it
2. It rained for-ty days, for-ty
3. A knock at the win - dow, a

1. rained for-ty nights There was-n't no land no-where in sights, God
2. nights with-out stopping No - ah was glad when the rain stopped dropping when
3. knock at the door They cried "Oh No - ah please take on more" But

1. sent   a   ra-ven to   bring the news   he hoist his   wings and a
2. I   get   to heav'n going to put   on my shoes   to walk 'round heav'n and
3. Noah cried   out that "You're full of   sin   my Lord's got   the key you

Copyright 1939 by Roberta Martin

TAKE MY HAND, PRECIOUS LORD

Chord names for Guitar
Symbols for Ukulele

Tune Uke
A D F# B

Words and Music by
THOMAS A. DORSEY

Copyright 1938 by Hill and Range Songs, Inc.
Copyright renewed 1965 and assigned to Hill and Range Songs, Inc.
Copyright 1951 by Hill and Range Songs, Inc., New York, N.Y.
International Copyright Secured   Printed in U.S.A.
All rights reserved including the right of public performance for profit

Be A Fence All Around Me

Arr. by Kenneth Morris

Words and Music by
SAM COOK

© Copyrighted 1962 by Kags Music, Los Angeles, Calif.
Exclusively distributed by Martin & Morris Music, Inc., 4812 Indiana Ave., Chicago, Ill., 60653

The Lord Will Make A Way Some How

A Dorsey Song   *As sung by Wilson Jubilee Singers, Cleveland, O.*

Leelis Wilson, Dir.

By THOMAS A. DORSEY

1 Like a ship thats toss'd and driv-en   Bat-tered by an ang-ry   sea
2 Try to do my best in ser - vice   Try to live the best I   can
3 Oft-en there's mis-und-er - stand-ing   Out of all the good I   do

When the storms of life are rag-ing And their fu - ry falls on me I
When I choose to do the right thing Ev - il's pres-ent on ev-'ry hand I
Go to friends for con-so - lat - ion And I find them com-plain-ing too So

won-der what I have done That makes this race so hard to run Then I
look up and won-der why That good for-tune pass me by Then I
man-y nights I toss in pain Won-der-ing what the day will bring But I

say to my soul take cou-rage
say to my soul be pat-ient   The Lord will make a way some how.
say to my heart don't wor-ry

BMI

CHORUS

The Lord will make a way some how
    some how,
When be-neath the cross I bow
    I bow

He will take a way each sor-row
    way each sor row,
Let Him have your bur-dens now
    all your bur-dens,

When the load bear down so hea-vy
    down so hea-vy,
The weight is shown up on my brow
    on my brow,

There's a sweet re-lief in know-ing O The Lord will make a way some how
    in know-ing, some-how.

I Find No Fault In Him

Words and Music by
ANDRAE CROUCH

© Copyright 1966 by MANNA MUSIC, INC.,
International Copyright Secured   Printed in U. S. A.
All rights reserved including the right of public performance for profit

What Lies Ahead? 8

The preceding chapters have set forth in some detail the story of the development of Black sacred music. The ground and root of all music indigenous to America is the music art form commonly known as the Negro Spiritual. (See the "Music Tree" on the frontispiece.) Its antecedents were the slave utterances, moans, and chants for deliverance that can be traced to the early slave experience. The Spiritual evolved from the rhythm forms of the West African oral tradition as a folk response to and index of the social dynamics and culture of the slave community. The oral tradition was the primary means of the Spiritual's survival and dissemination throughout the slave and folk community. In the course of the accommodation necessary in the New World, in the areas of religion, language, and mores, music revealed what was going on in the life of the antebellum slave community and registered the varied responses to servitude. Out of that response preserved chiefly in the Spiritual, there grew an identifiable Black musical tradition. This book has focused on the religious segment of the music of the Black experience and followed the sacred-secular distinctions of the West in order to present in bold relief the distinct tradition.

There is, then, a Black sacred music tradition that is identifiable and distinguishable from the sacred music tradition of the dominant (or White) society. It is obvious that the forms of celebration in the worship of the folk churches of the Black community and the Euro-American-influenced worship of the White community are vastly different. To be sure, as has been indicated earlier in this book, much of the language and trappings are similar, if not identical, but the style of the worship is markedly different. It does not require much analysis to discover that the chief influence and distinguishing ingredient is the music. The Black musical tradition, by its very character, induces a style of worship that lends itself to great freedom of expression. The music of the dominant society in worship is performed within the print-oriented strictures of the melodic and harmonic discipline common to the West. Improvisation is rare in White worship, and neither is there as widespread use of choirs and congregational singing.

Music is one of the key ingredients that influences the style of worship in Protestant church life in America. As stated in chapter 1, there are some Black congregations whose worship style is imitative of the dominant society and a key ingredient is, again, *the music.* In the worship services of the Black masses music plays very nearly as central a role as preaching. The reader may recall that the style of preaching and praying in the Black religious tradition was influenced by the music of the Black religious experience.

Similarities do exist between what might be called Black-style worship and White-style worship. The principal similarity is in language. While there is a great store of Black-rooted musical repertoire used, better than half of the printed music adapted for use in contemporary Black church life is Euro-American in origin. The first similarity, then, is in language. The second similarity is in the words. A traditional favorite and standard of any Black folk congregation is "Amazing Grace,"[1] authored by John Newton, an English slave trader turned Anglican priest.[2] However, the similarity is principally in the words, with only slight reference to the melodic line, when one compares the use and performance of this hymn in historic Black church life with the use and performance in White church life.

The form and style of Black sacred music generally followed the folk religion, that is, the religion of the masses, who are generally low income and rural in origin. Again, the folk religion of the Black community had naturally and inevitably felt some influence of the dominant society. But the folk-style religion has remained intact because the persistent thread of the oral tradition has preserved a musical idiom unique to the Black religious experience.

There are, of course, exceptions to the rule on both sides of this religious coin: some all-Black congregations sing like White folks, and a few White worship services are filled with the fervor of traditional Black religion, *but the music is not the same!* It might be argued that this is evidence of cross-cultural influence, to which this writer would hastily agree. Cross culture feeds and alters; it does not devour and destroy.

One additional observation might be added in this regard. The corollary to the fact of the existence of an observable Black sacred music tradition is that the dominance of that tradition *musically* is in direct proportion to the influence of the religious folk tradition. That is to say, the folk religion lives where the folk music is sung and *vice versa*. A converse truth prevails. As the influence of Euro-American music increases, the folk style religion decreases.

The Black Sacred Music Tradition

The existence of a Black sacred music tradition is made evident by the several types of music, still extant, that are utilized in varying degrees in the folk religion of the masses. In summary, let us retrace the bloodline of this body of musical literature.

The Spiritual is the name given to that body of music that developed from 1760 to the Emancipation (1863). It embraces the Sorrow Songs, Field Songs, Praise Songs, Shouts, Hollers, Work Songs, and the like. This musical art form was sufficiently developed by the beginning of the nineteenth century to color and transform the meter music tradition that had its roots in Europe. The Spiritual form had its impact on the use made of the Euro-American hymns that were introduced on a broad scale to the Black community following the Civil War. It was not long before the rhythm, mode, style, and ad-lib character of performance stamped Black America's imprint upon the music in question. The Hymns of Improvisation, as they have been named in this book, dominated the worship of historic Black churches until the hard times of the Great Depression, when the vogue of authentic Gospel music first appeared. The experience of placing their imprint on "borrowed" hymns created sufficient confidence internally for Blacks to produce their own Black hymnody—Gospel!

The advent of the Martin Luther King era of radical social change ushered in a period of broad acceptability of the Gospel idiom, which had not been altogether welcome in all-Black church circles prior to that time.[3] The nonviolent movement in the South, at its inception, "updated" many of the historic Negro Spirituals and transformed them through slight word changes into Freedom Songs.[4] As the movement gained momentum, with the broad popularity of Freedom Songs and the close similarity to their musical parents, the Spirituals, the door was opened for the most recent development in Black hymnody—Modern Gospel. Modern Gospel is a composite of the Black sacred music tradition. Its musical idiom is very often "bluesy" and/or jazzy. Its lyrics are traditional, either from the Euro-American tradition or variations on the faith language long existent in the Black religious experience. It is not uncommon in the worship service of a church of the Black masses to hear under the Gospel umbrella a selection that has elements of several of the types reviewed here. For example, the formula might take shape as follows: meter music + Gospel + Spiritual (text or verse) = Contemporary Gospel.

Lord, Don't Move the Mountain[5]

I love the Lord: he heard my cries,
    And pitied every groan:
Long as I live, when troubles rise,
    I'll hasten to his throne.[6]

Refrain

Lord, don't move the mountain;
Just give me the strength to climb.
Lord, don't take away my stumbling block;
Just lead me all around.[7]

Stanza (typical)

Lord, I don't bother nobody,
I try to treat everybody the same;
But every time I turn my back,
They scandalize my name.[8]

    The Spirituals, the Hymns of Improvisation, the Black meter music tradition, and Historic and Modern Gospel are the major forms of musical literature that comprise the Black sacred music tradition. Wherever the tradition has lived, measurable growth in personal and collective wholeness has proceeded.

The internal development of the Black community has centered in the Black Church institution, and the cohesive influence to a large degree has been the music of the Black religious tradition. The examples cited earlier in this regard are evidence of the long- and short-range positive influences and results that were made possible through the oral tradition that has permeated the development of Black sacred music. The music of the Black Church was crucial in the institution's development as the dominant influence in the life of the Black community, past and present.

Black Sacred Music and Social Change

Black sacred music is the primary link to the African past of the Black people in the Americas. It has survived against tremendous odds. Black sacred music could not and would not have survived without the instrumentality of the oral tradition. The illiteracy of the Black community (by Western standards) made the oral tradition essential. As the Black community became more westernized, the historic past of the New World African became more distant and obscured. The Western value system (color, economics, intellectualism) discourages a sense of "Negro" identity, but an irreducible minimum remains.

The Black community developed as an appendage to American society. Sociologists use the term "subculture." It was in Black religious life earlier on, and later in the church and the entertainment world, that Black expression was given vent without having to absorb the neutralizing effect of White nonacceptance.

Slavery and its successor, segregation, produced a psychological and emotional disorientation in Blacks that remains observable today. In their collective consciousness, the Black people have not been absolutely sure who they are. They are not thoroughly American; they are not thoroughly African. They move in an ambivalent world of being *Afro-American*.

The most positive neutralizing effect on this disorientation of identity came as a result of the nonviolent movement in the South and the intense but brief "Black Power" movement. Whatever happened, the primary and most significant result was the psychic impact these events had on Black consciousness. Both periods fed the gnawing need for identity and self-image that White America had sought to destroy through historical and cultural genocide. White America had made blackness taboo; Martin Luther King, Jr., Malcolm X, and Stokely Carmichael made it fashionable.

In the treatment of Jews and Blacks by White Americans there are sufficient similarities for instructive comparison. It is obvious that Jews have fared somewhat better for a couple of reasons. One reason is, of course, their "whiteness," which serves as a camouflage to their Jewishness in many circumstances. The other reason is their Jewishness—the mystique of the heirs of Moses who are remaining, generally, unapologetic for being Jews. This is buttressed by their separateness (religion) and their sense of exclusivity (chosen people). The Old Testament and the tradition of the Torah have done much to fortify and insulate the Jewish community from persecution and discrimination that might have demoralized a lesser people.

Sterling Plumpp in his book *Black Rituals* is more explicit as to how this Jewish mystique functions:

> The reason that Jews are so functional in mobilizing their strength all over the world when their survival is endangered is that Jews are unified. There are no Black men heading Jewish organizations, there are no Black critics telling Jews how to sing, what to write and how smart they are—only Jews define what a Jew is and how a Jew should and shouldn't act. Jewish culture is rooted in centuries of Jewish history. . . . What is very essential to any correct understanding of the "success" of the Jews in any country is the fact that they learn to play roles, wear many different masks, in order to make it, advance in technological and industrialized jungles. This means they learn how to act like Americans . . . but in their familiar religious institutions they also learn how to live as Jews must live if they are to survive; they learn this from the cradle.[9]

The irony of the Black people's sojourn on the North American continent is that as they have become more and more westernized—literate and elevated in economics and social status—they have become more removed from their real past. The continuing dilemma of Afro-Americans in the U.S. is to discover ways to resist complete Westernization which obliterates ethnic pride and identity. On the basis of the American experience, the Westernization mentioned above invariably induces the subject (victim) to join with the dominant (oppressive) community in its mores, life-style, and value system. This is notwithstanding the fact that Western culture. historically, has been anti-Black.

There is no indication of a mass exodus from America. Thus it is safe to presume that Black people will stay. If they remain, how can they keep their sanity? Imitate the Jewish experience? Well, at least learn from it.

The parallels of the Jewish and Black experiences are profoundly similar. In the Black ancestral home family life and religious life were central. The slave period disrupted that tradition but not totally. The historical umbilical cord needs to be rejoined. Plumpp has already underscored the importance of this influence in the survival technique of the Jewish community. The centrality of the family, synagogue, and tradition has served them well. Blacks must acquire the skills and expertise of the dominant society and at the same time preserve and strengthen ethnicity—Blackness. The basis of that preservation is grounded in a *sense of history*. The Jewish model is well worth considering as an option—an example of bicultural competence.

Blackamericans who dismiss the slave experience are foolish and short-sighted. This is not a brief for masochism. However, once the slave experience has been faced, more important questions arise: "What were we before we were slaves?" "What set of circumstances led to our enslavement?" "How did we survive and by what means?" The cloak of historic invisibility must be lifted from the collective and individual consciousness of American Blacks in order to cope with the reality of systemic White racism.

It has been set forth earlier in this book that the dominant institutional influence in the lives of Afro-Americans is the Black Church. The Black people's sense of personhood—being—has been nurtured and fed by the Black religious experience. The "invisible church" was the chief resistance movement against slavery. The "visible church" is uniquely equipped to serve as the instrument to awaken and reawaken the sense of history so sorely needed. The music of the Black religious experience has been and remains a reservoir of the Black community's response to enforced servitude and oppression. The music which developed from the basic idiom that survived the Middle Passage was fashioned into a cry for deliverance. Transmitted via the oral tradition of West Africa and adapted to the experience of the New World, this faith music provided the cement that held the fragile "invisible church" together until the organization of the "visible church" became possible.

The inhumanity of pre-Civil War existence was made bearable by the presence and function of the "invisible church." The religious beliefs, captured and preserved in song, transformed the property of the slave owners into the children of God.

The music of the Black religious experience in the folk tradition induces and reinforces a clearer sense of heritage. The quality of performance, style, beat, and emotion of Black worship assists Blacks in discovering and remembering who they really are.

The Spiritual form, in the antebellum style or post-Civil War style, in Black consciousness has always been associated with the slave experience. On at least four occasions since the act of emancipation, the Spiritual form has experienced a pronounced renaissance, both in interest and in use. Shortly after the executive order for emancipation was signed by Lincoln, the Spirituals lapsed into gradual neglect, only to be resurrected by the domestic and international tours of the Fisk Jubilee Singers. Then, at the beginning of the twentieth century, with the increased use of hymn texts, the use of Spirituals declined again until the John Work years (1914-1930). The period of the Great Depression saw still another decline in the popularity of Spirituals while the new "Gospel" music of the Black church began to take root. World War II, a time of national crisis, marked another renaissance led by the internationally famous Wings Over Jordan radio choir,[10] based in Cleveland, Ohio. As America wound down from World War II prosperity, interest in the Spiritual waned again, in deference to the Gospel era which now held full sway. The fifties could be accurately called the era of the quartet phenomenon, so strong was this phase of the Gospel movement.

The meteoric rise of Martin Luther King, Jr., and the stirring movement against the racist forces in the South created still another renaissance. The heightening of the collective Black consciousness and the marching feet needed music to bolster the morale of Blacks and give them courage. Martin King was a Baptist preacher; the movement that he led was church-based; the most suitable music for this moral struggle was the music of the antebellum slave who one hundred years earlier intoned:

> Go down, Moses,
> Way down in Egypt land.

Tell ole Pharaoh,
Let my people go.[11]

God had sent another Moses to lift the affliction of slavery from the oppressed. Their song in a strange land was the Lord's song coined generations earlier by their slave forebears. The Spirituals were in business again!

As detailed earlier in this book, the Freedom Songs (contemporized Spirituals) gave the Spiritual art form its broadest acceptance. The impact of television and instantaneous news reporting was of no small importance in this regard. The entire nonviolent movement was religious in tone, and the music did much to reflect and reinforce the religious base on which it stood. In the course of its development, the movement drew into its wake many people who were nonreligious, irreligious, and antireligious, but singing Freedom Songs for them and for others of diverse persuasions was a means of comfortable participation. It was this development which contributed most to minimizing the distinction between sacred and secular within the Black music tradition. The evolution of Freedom Songs and the impact of rhythm and blues prepared most of the ground in which Modern Gospel grew.

All of this review only serves to illustrate again the relationship between music and crisis in the Black community. Since the chief repository of authentic Black religious music remains in the church, and the church collectively attracts the largest segment of the Black community, it follows, then, that the music of the Black religious tradition can be a vital instrument for a ministry of social change. The Black Church has the troops and the inspiring music. The music of the Black religious tradition operates on two levels: first, psychologically and emotionally—it locates the people's sense of heritage, their roots, where they are and where they want to go; and secondly, it mobilizes and strengthens the resolve for struggle. A people's sense of destiny is rooted in their sense of history. Black sacred music is the primary reservoir of the Black people's historical context and an important factor in the process of social change.

The preceding paragraph might seem "visionary" or at least presumptuous. However, when one considers the hostile context and arduous route of development of Black sacred music, deference must be accorded its track record.

The enslavement of Black people in this republic and the cruelties that have accompanied it approach the unspeakable. Yet the Black community, for the most part, emerged with its humanity intact. Eugene Genovese, a Marxist, spent eleven years studying the slave system; and his recent monumental work, *Roll, Jordan, Roll,* concludes that Black people's religion was the means of their survival.[12] Aside from Genovese's corroborating conclusion which church-oriented Blacks have always known, it is interesting that he titled his important work with a Spiritual.[13] Part and parcel of that survival documented in his book is the crucial role of the faith music in preserving the personhood of the New World African. The Spirituals, root of the Black sacred music tradition, kept the small flames burning on the heart altars of an oppressed people. The several facets of the Spirituals' instrumentality in this regard have been delineated. The specific uses, over and above the general importance of Spirituals to the slave community, are illustrated by their use as a signal for Nat Turner's rebellion, the jailing of Blacks in Georgetown, South Carolina, for singing of freedom,[14] and the frequent use of Spirituals made in the days of the Underground Railroad.[15]

Without the body of music that was born and transmitted orally across the South from plantation to plantation and town to town, the "invisible church" that followed the Emancipation Proclamation would not have survived. The musical phenomenon of Black religion was the primary support system of the developmental period of historic Black churches. These same churches and the denominations they have produced (African Methodist Episcopal, African Methodist Episcopal Zion, National Baptist Convention, Inc., National Baptist Convention of U.S.A., Christian Methodist Episcopal, Progressive National Baptist Convention) have all benefited in their growth and development from the cohesive influence of Black sacred music. Very little serious argument can be found to deny the maxim "As goes Black music, so goes the Black Church."

In more recent days the central role of music of the Black religious experience has been more clearly demonstrated. Who can deny that the nonviolent movement of the sixties did more for raising the consciousness level of the Black *and* White communities in America on the issue of justice than any other set of events since Emancipation? An integral part of the whole process of radical social change, primarily in the South, was the music of the Black religious experience.

> It is safe to say that the Freedom Movement in the South is a "singing Movement." This is somewhat to be expected when one considers that music has strange power to evoke various emotional responses in the human animal. It has, historically, been of special value to the oppressed in every age. Somehow, the literature and idiom of music makes possible the restoration of lost hopes, it binds up the wounds of the broken-hearted, and by its character welds together the cohesive sentiment of a group of people of common experience.[16]

In point of specific reference:

> It is perfectly clear that the recent nonviolent thrust of the Negro community might not have had the vitality and dynamism that it has were it not for the impact of the Negro spiritual. The natural response to music, coupled with the deep meaning of the Negro spiritual, has produced a unique effect on the Freedom Movement in the South. It must always be remembered that religious orientation of the Freedom Movement intensifies the effect produced. Perhaps it should be said that the Freedom Movement's natural character of being religiously orientated is inseparable from the effect of . . . the Negro spiritual. They are each a supplement of the other.[17]

As a participant for nearly a decade in the nonviolent movement in the South, most of the time in the front lines, this writer is thoroughly convinced that there would have been very little "movement" without the music of the Black religious tradition. The author crisscrossed the South from Virginia to Texas, winter and summer, spring and fall, and there was no *movement* that did not sing the music of the Black religious tradition.[18]

One other excerpt documents this commonality:

> How has the Negro spiritual served the Freedom Movement in the South? . . . it is no mystery that with the Negro community's social life focused in the church and his protest movements religiously oriented, it would follow that the music of the movement similarly would be that which is most informal and expressive of the deep yearnings of the ethnic group from which it has sprung.[19]

Most knowledgeable chroniclers of the Martin Luther King era consider Birmingham as one of the chief watersheds of the nonviolent movement in the South. In January of 1963, the late John F. Kennedy met with the heads of the major civil rights groups and indicated that he felt there was sufficient legislation on the issue of civil rights. In June of the same year, in a network radio and television address, he pleaded with America to face this "moral crisis," as he introduced what was to become the Civil Rights Act of 1964 (Public Accommodations Bill).[20] This radical change in presidential posture is directly attributable to the historic confrontation in Birmingham in the spring of that same year. Of course, there were several necessary ingredients that made the Birmingham movement the huge success that it was, and chief among these was the fact that the Birmingham movement was a great singing movement.

Most of the key figures were handsomely skilled song leaders. Andrew Young, Dorothy Cotton, James Bevel, Fred Shuttlesworth, and Bernard Lee were accomplished song leaders, and none was better than Ralph Abernathy.[21]

A standard technique of the movement was to move the mass meetings from community to community in order to encourage support and provide accurate information. It is important to note that on the very day that demonstrations were launched in Birmingham, after three postponements (stretching from November, 1962, to April 3, 1963), the city bus system went on strike. Without public transportation, it was thought that the infant movement was doomed. Yet for thirty-nine nights, without interruption, the rallies were held in support of one of the most significant struggles in the South. A great deal of the stimulus for the sustained rallies was the quality of the music that made the mass meetings attractive in spite of the transportation dilemma.

Birmingham was not the only outstanding "singing movement." Equally distinctive in quality and fervor were the two Albany, Georgia, campaigns (1961), Nashville, Tennessee (1960), Petersburg, Virginia (1960), and, of course, the "granddaddy of them all," the Montgomery, Alabama, bus protest, 1955–1956.[22]

The strength of the movement was mobilized and programmed through the instrumentality of Black sacred music. The great churches, both in influence and in size, came to their positions of prominence with the heavy influence of the music of the Black religious tradition. The large numbers of people gravitated toward the music that was familiar to their experience and spoke to their hearts and souls.

The Continuing Importance of Black Sacred Music

The present moment in Black church life is one of severe crisis. The high-speed events of the last fifteen years in social change (much of it church sponsored and/or church led) have raised measurably the expectations of the Black and oppressed community. As the backlash sets in as a response to the identifiable gains made in recent years, the combination of events has placed an awesome challenge on the doorstep of the Black Church which it is hard pressed to answer. The virtue of having been the dominant influence in the life of the oppressed community has seemingly been distorted into cardinal sin. Many strident voices, outside and inside the church are asking, "What have you done for me lately?" Pointing to the record of yester-year is insufficient to slough the persistent criticism leveled at the Black Church. It is undeniably true that the humanity of Black people could never have survived without their Africanized Christianity. The record speaks for itself. Nonetheless, James Russell Lowell said in poetic verse, "Time makes ancient good uncouth."[23]

It's a new age so far as the expectancy of the oppressed community is concerned, and it looks, properly so, to that institution which has been the chief liberating influence in its history. There are about fourteen million people of African descent in the various denominations across the United States, and the onus is upon the Black Church to give an account of its impact on Black life commensurate with its resources and the age in which it purports to serve. The very survival of the Black community can be directly attributed to the role that the Black Church has played in the lives of the people it served, but this can be no excuse to rest on its laurels of past performance.

Given the Black condition in America, the Black Church has a greater potential for a ministry of social change than does any other quarter of Black life. The cruel irony of this moment in history is that at the very instant the oppressed community's expectancy is highest, the climate in the republic is such that the likelihood of realization is lowest. The harsh reality of American life for the Black people is that as far as the delivery of services, employment, quality education, income dollars, housing, and such are concerned, they are worse off now than they were prior to the Supreme Court decision of 1954. This is no denial of gains made during what has been termed the King era, but for the most part the gains have been symbolic and not substantive. The great masses of Black people have been untouched by the societal changes that have been so visible. It follows, then, that calculated efforts must be made to maximize the liberating influence of the Black Church enterprise in the lives of the people it serves.

How shall the Black Church proceed? It is an oversimplification to say that the Black Church must serve this dilemma-ridden generation just as the "invisible church" served its generation. The enemy is the same; only his methods have changed. What can the Black Church do? It can remain as the citadel of hope and faith to a people too long oppressed, and in this generation it can try to create a model that delivers twentieth-century answers to twentieth-century problems. The injunction of the Galilean Prince is timeless and timely: "Feed the hungry, clothe the naked, heal the sick, give shelter to the homeless, bind up the wounds of the brokenhearted, set at liberty the captives, and preach the good news to the poor." (See Matthew 25:35-38; Luke 4:18.)

The Black Church cannot do it all, but it can *begin!* Much of the criticism against the present-day Black Church is unwarranted, but some of it has legitimate grounds. The energy of the Black Church is too precious to be spent making defenses; it must address itself to correcting and strengthening the areas of its responsibility which are under legitimate attack. There is no way, generally or specifically, that the Black Church can function in the real world of the American nightmare without the instruments of the struggle: a *theology grounded in liberation,* a *contemporary sense of historical context,* a *God-ordained sense of destiny in this land,* and the *determination to endure.* Each of the above could require an inquiry in the context of the Black experience in America. They are listed here as ingredients which are contained in the music of the Black religious tradition. It is a very short step to conclude that maximizing the potential of the Black Church enterprise can be facilitated best through the use of its primary culture vehicle—Black sacred music!

It is obvious, then, that the first step for any congregation that is genuinely interested in a ministry of social change is to preserve the integrity of the Black sacred music tradition. That is to say, churches peopled by the oppressed community must be diligent in resisting the temptation to "improve" so much that the musical idiom which helped them to survive is lost or diluted beyond recognition.

Music is central in Black worship and thus is the real index of where a people are religiously and culturally. If Black churches lose their unique and distinctive musical idiom, then those same Black churches will be culturally and religiously out of context. The temptation to sing "good" music within the aura of urban churches with robed clergy and choirs, printed orders of worship, and the like is real. Stringent measures must be taken to preserve the integrity of the cultural vehicle, Black sacred music in this instance, so that the sense of history so crucial to an oppressed people is not destroyed. In many ways it is not an overstatement to say that Black music is the Black experience, whether it is secular or sacred.

The foregoing is not a brief for a total Black experience worship style. This is neither necessary nor desirable. Black people in America are not altogether American *culturally* or altogether African *culturally*. As they are biracial in most instances, they are also bicultural. They speak the language of the realm; they are acculturated to the mores via religion and custom; they have adopted, to a large degree (unfortunately) the value system of the dominant society. Black people are probably more American than they are African. But the African influence is present, and its presence has been an important ingredient for Black people culturally and more especially musically. Through their music, Black people have made a singular contribution to Americana. It is very likely that if the integrity of Black music is maintained, they may, as well, make a singular contribution religiously by restoring to America its humanity. The religion of America is far removed from the substantive ethic of the Lord Jesus Christ. Reinhold Niebuhr states that Christianity in America has been corrupted into the manifest destiny of the nation. Things have become more important than people. When one reviews the agenda of the White and Black churches in America, the Black Church has been generally much closer to the concerns of the Galilean Prince than its White counterpart.

There is no need or desire to exclude the Western influence from the Black people's life-style but, rather, to make use of the most positive of those influences to give clearer expression in the American context to their own particular cultural genius. Black people are American like all other ethnic groups—Irish, German, Italian, or

Polish—and like all others, they are no less American because they preserve the ethnicity of culture and ancestry. In the religious arena this translates directly to developing the Black Church into an up-to-date institution that meets the challenges of the era with equanimity, without any loss of its cultural or ethnic identity. This means a Church with the very best equipment and resources that it can acquire. without any abridgment of its commitment to maintain the integrity of the Black community's unique and peculiar odyssey on these shores.

It is not enough to accept intellectually the concept of developing a bicultural stance in the central communal act of worship. The concept must take on a consciousness that gives flesh and sinew to programmatic development aimed at *maintaining the integrity of the cultural vehicle* (including the music of the Black religious tradition) and at the same time produce a bicultural stance reflective of the real world in which the Black Church exists.

The first step is a clear understanding and definition of what this cultural vehicle is and whence it has come. It is hoped that this book and other related materials would serve as a base for this first step. The maximum use of Black sacred music cannot be even approximated without an understanding and appreciation of what the instrument is. Secondly, at the individual church level at least and, one would hope, at denominational and educational levels as well, a conscious decision must be made to preserve the musical idiom of the Black religious experience. It will not suffice for any such program to move on the charisma of the pastor who may be gone next week. An unsympathetic successor can undo in five months what a predecessor has labored five years to develop. The conscious decision might well take the form of a church resolution of policy, acted upon by the entire body that says in substance, "We will be true to our heritage and preserve the musical idiom of our forefathers, whose faith has brought us as far as we have come." This step is buttressed by conveying to musicians employed by the congregation that the use of Black sacred music in all of its traditional forms (in conjunction with Euro-American music) is a matter of *church policy*.

The next step may be troublesome. Good musicians cost money. The effective development of a musical program with a pronounced bicultural stance will not proceed with a church policy statement alone. It must have the parallel *budget* commitment. Church musicians generally have received short shrift for any number of reasons too varied to list here. The primary reason is low-budget priority. It will become the responsibility of church leadership to see to it that the companion budget commitment is made attendant to the policy commitment.

All of the above helps to put the train on the track. The task is still far from complete. One must not underestimate the strong and persistent pull of Western influences that threaten to dilute or supplant that which has given "staying power" to the Black Church community. A conscious and deliberate program such as that outlined above will need buttressing of several sorts. In the historic Black churches there is no substitute for "pulpit stress." Many worthwhile and well-conceived programs in church life fail and drift into the sunset solely because "Rev." didn't provide adequate pulpit support. Silence from the pulpit has killed many a project aborning.

In that same vein, announcements are helpful and supportive, but preaching maintains a high priority. There is an inexhaustible mine for serious and creative preaching in Black sacred music. The intense, personal identification with Black hymnody is such that it cannot help giving fresh meaning to the everyday experiences of the worshipers. Sermon series can be effective and productive. The spiritual insights of the Spirituals and other types of Black hymnody are so profound that those insights lend themselves to contemporary preaching. The possibilities are enormous with the choir(s) tied in directly to the theme of the minister's preaching.

Add to the sermonic efforts music workshops aimed at and focused on Black hymnody, Gospel festivals, and Black culture series, with dramatic presentations that tell the story of the music of the Black religious experience. In urban centers, especially though not exclusively, the tradition of fellowship or exchange services might be used for joint programs built around the theme of the music of the Black religious experience. Some communities sponsor such festivals on a citywide basis. Those congregations that have adequate resources and competent choirs often record. Thus, in an informal and sometimes commercial way, they continue the musical idiom that so far has been preserved chiefly through the oral tradition that has tenaciously persisted in Black Church life.

Figure 15

Town Hall, Friday Evening, November 15, 1974 at 8:00 p.m.

CANAAN BAPTIST CHURCH OF CHRIST
The Rev. Dr. Wyatt T. Walker, Minister
presents

CLINTON H. UTTERBACH

AND

THE RECORDING CHOIR

In

"RISE UP AND WALK"

A MUSICAL TRIBUTE TO ALL THE HEROES OF
THE BLACK STRUGGLE FOR FREEDOM

EUGENE COOPER, *Organist*   CLARENCE STROMAN, *Drums*
ROBERT HARGROVE, *Organist*   EARL WALKER, *Bass Guitar*
NAOMI THOMAS, *Pianist*   WILLIAM ALLEN, *Bass Guitar*

CLINTON H. UTTERBACH, *Writer/Conductor*

Creation

HE DOTH ALL THINGS WELL .... Carolyn Byrd Allen
GREAT AND MARVELOUS .... Choir (Henry Farmer)

Of Bondage

SOMETIMES I FEEL LIKE A MOTHERLESS CHILD . . Rubena Parker
SOON WILL BE DONE .... Clint Utterbach & Carolyn Byrd Allen

Of Hope

TROUBLE IN DE LAND .... Choir
DIDN'T MY LORD DELIVER DANIEL .... Beaulah Johnson &
                                                    Vivian Ross
WASN'T THAT A WIDE RIVER ....

"Rise Up and Walk," an original music-narrative, written and directed by Clinton Utterbach, depicts the struggle for freedom in word and song. A sample of Harlem church life came alive on Broadway and provided an evening of culture and entertainment to an appreciative "standing room only" audience. (See Figure 15.)

There is one other touchstone that is directly related to the matter of keeping the integrity of Black sacred music. It has to do with the impact of Black hymnody and the Euro-American use of hymnody. It is observable in the level of participation. White congregations tend to be more spectator oriented, while Black congregations tend to be more participant oriented. The contrast is between a "proper" worship stance and the verbal free expression in Black churches. Depending upon the roots of the music, this distinguishing feature is true of secular music as well. There is a direct connection between this distinguishing feature of Black and White hymnody and the experiential versus rational character of Black and White worship. Churches that are heavily Euro-American in their worship style tend to celebrate the rational: the worship in non-European churches tends to celebrate the experiential *as well as* the rational.

Thus, the flavor of the worship celebration is determined largely by which mode obtains. White-style services are shorter, more rigid in worship form, and less emotional, and the music is conformity oriented. On the other hand, Black-style worship is of longer duration, less formal and less rigid, emotion filled, and expression oriented. Authentic Black-style worship does not proceed without frequent exhortations of "Amen," "Tell the Truth," "Say it," "Preach, brother," "Sing your song," and the like. Without signal, an entire congregation will join with a soloist at a peak moment in the rendition. Black-style worship, if it is anything, is a spontaneous communal celebration affirming God's presence and activity in the individual and collective lives of the worshipers.

Beyond the worship experience, the deeper concern is the impact observable in the everyday life of the oppressed community. Of what value is the music of the Black religious experience in the personal and collective lives of the people themselves?

The significance of the impact of the music of the Black religious tradition is broad. Given the dilemma of Black people in America, it is a marvel of religion that great numbers actively pursue a faith in

God. The abundance and variety of religious experiences within the Black Protestant Christian tradition context is demonstrative of the vitality of that faith. There are few, if any, Black churches on the American scene closing, or merging, in order to survive. Whatever the genius of the Black Church that keeps its members' hopes alive, Black sacred music plays a central role.

The devices of the music are many. Black people have always lived in a state of emergency. They are a crisis people. Their history is punctuated with trials and tribulations of every color and hue. Yet Blacks have survived. The music of faith, especially the Spirituals, mirrors the social context of the Black people's travail in this land. Consequently, Black sacred music in the worship celebration calls forth recollections personally and collectively of past hardships and victories over trouble. The message of the music reminds the burdened of today that just as "God delivered Daniel in the lions' den," so would they be delivered from the afflictions of this life.

The music of the Black church often verbalized poetically that which the individual has difficulty articulating. It is not uncommon to hear, in the everyday speech of the faithful, the idiomatic use of snatches of lines of hymns and Spirituals. The religion of Black Christians is so largely encouched in their musical tradition that the verbiage is familiar to all, young and old. A common response to the courtesy greeting, "How are you?" is very often, "I'm holding on," a shortening of the Gospel hymn title "I'm Just Holding On." When some occurrence takes place that smacks of good fortune, a frequent response in explanation is, "It pays to serve Jesus *every day.*" Much of this idiomatic usage of the music language is a spinoff from the heavy use of hymn lyrics in preaching. One practice reinforces the other, and the singing of the music strengthens both.

The music of the Black religious experience was born and developed and shaped in a specific social context of suffering and oppression. Thus, the recollection of past trials through which God sustained and/or delivered his children strengthens the faith of the believer. Harlem is a very difficult place to keep one's faith in God. The widespread church life among Blacks and the concomitant activity that goes on is evidence that the people who comprise the congregations of the Harlems of this land are continually renewing their faith.

Much of the morale building necessary to faith renewal is traceable to the impact and influence of Black hymnody in the life of the individual worshiper. Church members who frequent night services in the inner city or weeknight activities are adamant about the inherent dangers of the crime-ridden streets. They earnestly believe that "God will take care of you."[24] In spite of muggings and burgled apartments, choir members and officers and lay members keep Black Church life alive by their tenacious resolve. Much of the fear quotient is drained away in the Sunday worship celebrations and weekday meetings that strengthen their resolve. Central in both is the broad use of the music of the Black religious experience. One other important aspect of Black hymnody's impact on the life of the congregation is its unifying influence. People are diverse by nature; yet the Black Church enterprise is the *prima facie* example of the Black people's cooperative effort in the face of adversity. There is no need to set forth again the crucial importance of music in the development of the Black church, but it is important to suggest the psychological basis for that success story. It is grounded in both the medium (singing) and the circumstance (oppression). Within the faith-worship context, the physical act of singing collectively in response to problems that are *collective* and *individual* expresses a commonality of circumstance that induces a sense of unity. It is very possible and probable that the input of the music at this level contributed significantly to the growth and development of the Black Church enterprise. All of the available evidence argues strongly that the music of the Black religious experience is inseparably intertwined with the origin, growth, and development of the Black Church as we know it today.

The Black Church of the future must seriously and systematically preserve, develop, and utilize this rich resource if it is to engage in service commensurate with both its past history and its future challenges. And when the oppression is over and the experiences have leveled off, Black sacred music *will* be one of the gifts of Black people to the Church universal, both here and hereafter.

Selected Bibliography

Bennett, Lerone, Jr., *Before the Mayflower: A History of the Negro in America, 1619–1964,* rev. ed. Baltimore: Penguin Books, 1966.

Blassingame, John W., *The Slave Community.* New York: Oxford University Press, 1972.

Boatner, Edward, *Spirituals Triumphant: Old And New.* Nashville: Sunday School Publishing Board, National Baptist Convention, U.S.A., 1927.

Brink, William, and Harris, Louis, *The Negro Revolution in America.* New York: Simon & Schuster, Inc., 1969.

Cone, James H., *The Spirituals and the Blues: An Interpretation.* New York: The Seabury Press, Inc., 1972.

Courlander, Harold, *Negro Folk Music, U.S.A.* New York: Columbia University Press, 1963.

Davidson, Basil, *The African Past.* New York: Grossett & Dunlap, Inc., 1967.

Davis, Ruth Lomax et al., *The New National Baptist Hymnal,* 3rd ed. Nashville: National Baptist Publishing Board, 1978.

De Lerma, Dominique-Rene, *Black Music in Our Culture.* Kent, Ohio: Kent State University Press, 1970.

Dett, R. Nathaniel, *Religious Folk Songs of the Negro.* Hampton, Va.: Hampton Institute Press, 1927.

Du Bois, W. E. Burghardt, *The Souls of Black Folk.* New York: Washington Square Press, 1970.

Fisher, Miles Mark, *Negro Slave Songs in the United States.* Ithaca, N.Y.: Cornell University Press, 1953.

Fogel, Robert William, and Engerman, Stanley L., *Time on the Cross: The Economics of American Negro Slavery.* Boston: Little, Brown and Company, 1974.

Franklin, John Hope, *From Slavery to Freedom,* 3rd ed. New York: Alfred A. Knopf, Inc., 1967.

Genovese, Eugene D., *Roll, Jordan, Roll.* New York: Pantheon Books, div. of Random House, 1974.

Heilbut, Tony, *The Gospel Sound: Good News and Bad Times.* New York: Simon & Schuster, Inc., 1971.

Herskovits, Melville J., *The Myth of the Negro Past.* New York: Harper & Row, Publishers, 1941.

Jahn, Janheinz, *Muntu.* New York: Grove Press, Inc., 1961.

Johnson, James Weldon, and Johnson, J. Rosamond, *The Books of American Negro Spirituals.* New York: A Viking Compass Book, imprint of The Viking Press, 1969.

Jones, Leroi [Amiri Baraka], *Black Music.* New York: William Morrow & Company, Inc., 1967.

Krehbiel, H. E., *Afro-American Folksongs.* New York: Frederick Ungar Publishing Co., 1962.

Lincoln, C. Eric, *The Black Church Since Frazier.* Bound with *The Negro Church in America* by E. Franklin Frazier. New York: Schocken Books, Inc., 1973.

Locke, Alain, *The Negro and His Music* and *Negro Art: Past and Present.* New York: Arno Press, Inc., 1969.

Logan, Rayford W., *The Betrayal of the Negro.* New York: Collier Books, 1965.

Lovell, John, Jr., *Black Song: The Forge and the Flame.* New York: Macmillan, Inc., 1972.

Mays, Benjamin E., *The Negro's God: As Reflected in His Literature.* New York: Atheneum Publishers, 1969.

Mbiti, John S., *African Religions and Philosophy.* Garden City, N.Y.: Anchor Books, Doubleday & Company, Inc., 1970.

Quarles, Benjamin, *The Negro in the Making of America,* rev. ed. New York: Collier Books, 1969.

Raboteau, Albert J., *Slave Religion.* New York: Oxford University Press, 1978.

Roach, Hildred, *Black American Music: Past and Present.* Boston: Crescendo Publishing Co., 1973.

Rublowsky, John, *Black Music in America.* New York: Basic Books, Inc., Publishers, 1971.

Southern, Eileen, *The Music of Black Americans: A History.* New York: W. W. Norton & Company, Inc., 1971.

Thurman, Howard, "The Meaning of Spirituals," in *International Library of Negro Life and History: The Negro in Music and Art,* compiled and edited by Lindsay Patterson. New York: Publishers Company, Inc., 1969.

Walker, Wyatt T., "The Soulful Journey of the Negro Spiritual: Freedom's Song," *Negro Digest,* July, 1963.

Walton, Ortiz, *Music: Black, White and Blue.* New York: William Morrow & Company, Inc., 1972.

Webber, Thomas L., *Deep Like the Rivers.* New York: W. W. Norton & Co., 1978.

Whalum, Wendel Phillips, "Black Hymnody," *Review and Expositor,* vol. 70, no. 3 (Summer, 1973).

Wilmore, Gayraud S., *Black Religion and Black Radicalism.* Garden City, N.Y.: Doubleday & Company, Inc., 1972.

Notes

Chapter 2

[1] Melville J. Herskovits, *The Myth of the Negro Past* (New York: Harper & Row, Publishers, 1941), pp. 213-224.

[2] See Lerone Bennett, Jr., *Before the Mayflower: A History of the Negro in America, 1619–1964,* rev. ed. (Baltimore: Penguin Books, 1966), p. 189.

[3] *Ibid.,* p. 240.

[4] John Hope Franklin, *From Slavery to Freedom,* 3rd ed. (New York: Alfred A. Knopf, Inc., 1967), pp. 404-406.

[5] United States Census, 1950.

[6] Franklin, *op. cit.,* p. 562.

[7] Benjamin Quarles, *The Negro in the Making of America,* rev. ed. (New York: Collier Books, imprint of Macmillan, Inc., 1969), p. 162.

[8] Wyatt Tee Walker, "Joseph Sizoo Memorial Lectures," New York Theological Seminary, March 1-3, 1974.

Chapter 3

[1] Hildred Roach, *Black American Music: Past and Present* (Boston: Crescendo Publishing Co., 1973), p. 9.

[2] *Ibid.,* p. 3.

[3] C. L. R. James, quoted in John Lovell, Jr., *Black Song: The Forge and the Flame* (New York: Macmillan, Inc., 1972), p. 64.

[4] John W. Blassingame, *The Slave Community* (New York: Oxford University Press, 1972), pp. 7-9.

[5] *Ibid.,* pp. 7, 9.

[6] *Ibid.,* p. 2.

[7] John Lovell, Jr., "The Social Implications of the Negro Spiritual," in *The Social Implications of Early Negro Music in the United States,* edited by

Bernard Katz (New York: Arno Press and The New York Times, 1969), p. 131.

8 Ortiz Walton, *Music: Black, White and Blue* (New York: William A. Morrow & Company, Inc., 1972), p. 22.

9 Lovell, *Black Song: The Forge and the Flame,* p. 69. Copyright © 1972 by John Lovell, Jr.

10 C. Eric Lincoln, "The Development of Black Religion in America," *Review and Expositor,* vol. 70, no. 3 (Summer, 1973), pp. 305-306.

11 Blassingame, *op. cit.,* p. 64.

12 Lovell, *Black Song: The Forge and the Flame,* p. 381.

13 Eileen Southern, *The Music of Black Americans: A History* (New York: W. W. Norton & Co., Inc., 1971), p. 216.

14 Lovell, "Social Implications," pp. 134-135.

15 Wendel Phillips Whalum, "Black Hymnody," *Review and Expositor,* vol. 70, no. 3 (Summer, 1973), p. 342.

16 Lovell, *Black Song: The Forge and the Flame,* pp. 118-119.

17 Whalum, *op. cit.,* p. 341.

18 *Ibid.,* p. 342.

19 Lovell, *Black Song: The Forge and the Flame,* p. 37.

20 Roach, *op. cit.,* p. 26.

21 Harry A. Ploski and Ernest Kaiser, *Afro, USA: A Reference Work on the Black Experience* (New York: Bellwether Publishing Company, Inc., 1971), p. 344; and Eileen Southern, *The Music of Black America: A History* (New York: W. W. Norton & Co., Inc., 1971), p. 105.

Chapter 4

1 Hildred Roach, *Black American Music: Past and Present* (Boston: Crescendo Publishing Co., 1973), p. 9.

2 Eileen Southern, *The Music of Black America: A History* (New York: W. W. Norton & Co., Inc., 1971), pp. 59, 146.

3 John Lovell, Jr., *Black Song: The Forge and the Flame* (New York: Macmillan, Inc., 1972), p. 111.

4 Maud Cuney Hare, "The Source," in *International Library of Negro Life and History: The Negro in Music and Art,* compiled and edited by Lindsay Patterson (New York: Publishers Company, Inc., 1969), pp. 19-30.

5 Zora Neale Hurston, "Spirituals and Neo-Spirituals," in *International Library of Negro Life and History,* p. 15.

6 John Rublowsky, *Black Music in America* (New York: Basic Books, Inc., Publishers, 1971), p. 41.

7 Kenneth Stampp, quoted in *ibid.,* p. 92.

8 Rublowsky, *op. cit.,* pp. 58-60.

9 *Ibid.,* p. 61.

10 Robert William Fogel and Stanley L. Engerman, *Time on the Cross: The*

Economics of American Negro Slavery (Boston: Little, Brown & Company, 1974), pp. 4-6.

[11] *Ibid.*, p. 9.

[12] *Ibid.*, p. 127.

[13] Wendel Phillips Whalum, "Black Hymnody," *Review and Expositor*, vol. 70, no. 3 (Summer, 1973), p. 341.

[14] Roach, *op. cit.*, p. 26.

[15] Whalum, *op. cit.*, p. 342.

[16] Lovell, *op. cit.*, p. 198.

[17] Harold Courlander, *Negro Folk Music, U.S.A.* (New York: Columbia University Press, 1963), p. 37.

[18] W. E. Burghardt Du Bois, *The Souls of Black Folk* (New York: Washington Square Press, 1970), p. 206.

[19] Hare, *op. cit.*, p. 19.

[20] Du Bois, *op. cit.*, pp. 208-209.

[21] Lovell, *op. cit.*, p. 63.

[22] Melville J. Herskovits, *The Myth of the Negro Past* (New York: Harper & Row, Publishers, 1941), chapters 6 and 7.

[23] Lovell, *op. cit.*, pp. 60, 65-68. Lovell lists Herskovits, Alan Lomax, Swami Parampanthi, J. Stanislav, Joseph Kyagambiddwa et al.

[24] *Ibid.*, p. 68.

[25] Roach, *op. cit.*, p. 8.

[26] Rublowsky, *op. cit.*, pp. 50-52.

[27] *Ibid.*, p. 52.

[28] Lovell, *op. cit.*, p. 69.

[29] Howard Thurman, "The Meaning of Spirituals," in *International Library of Negro Life and History*, p. 3.

[30] Miles Mark Fisher, *Negro Slave Songs in the United States* (Ithaca, N.Y.: Cornell University Press, 1953), pp. 41, 44, 144, 156, 161, 174.

[31] Benjamin E. Mays, *The Negro's God: As Reflected in His Literature* (New York: Atheneum Publishers, 1968), pp. 23-24.

[32] Thurman, *op. cit.*, p. 3.

[33] James H. Cone, *The Spirituals and the Blues: An Interpretation* (New York: The Seabury Press, Inc., 1972), chapter 3.

[34] Lovell, *op. cit.*, p. 223.

[35] Du Bois, *op. cit.*, pp. 208-209.

[36] Cone, *op. cit.*, p. 19.

[37] Thurman, *op. cit.*, pp. 3-8.

[38] Lovell, *op. cit.*, pp. 301, 304, 306, 310, 312, 314.

[39] Mary A. Grissom, *The Negro Sings a New Heaven* (New York: Dover Publications, Inc., 1969), table of contents.

[40] Wyatt T. Walker, "The Soulful Journey of the Negro Spiritual: Freedom's Song," *Negro Digest*, July, 1963.

[41] Lovell, *op. cit.*, p. 235.

[42] *Ibid.*, p. 273.

200 • "Somebody's Calling My Name"

[43] James Weldon Johnson and J. Rosamond Johnson, *The Books of American Negro Spirituals* (New York: A Viking Compass Book, imprint of The Viking Press, 1969), Book II, pp. 90-92.

[44] *Ibid.,* Book I, pp. 51-53.

[45] *Ibid.,* Book II, pp. 136-137.

[46] *Ibid.,* Book II, p. 30.

[47] *Southland Spirituals* (Chicago: The Rodeheaver Hall-Mack Co., 1936), p. 3.

[48] Johnson and Johnson, *op. cit.,* Book I, p. 134.

[49] Lovell, *op. cit.,* p. 46.

[50] Roach, *op. cit.,* pp. 28-29.

[51] Courlander, *op. cit.,* p. 42.

[52] Cone, *op. cit.,* p. 30.

[53] Whalum, *op. cit.,* p. 352.

[54] *Ibid.*

[55] Southern, *op. cit.,* p. 282.

[56] Roach, *op. cit.,* p. 111.

[57] Whalum, *op. cit.,* p. 353.

Chapter 5

[1] Wendel Phillips Whalum, "Black Hymnody," *Review and Expositor,* vol. 70, no. 3 (Summer, 1973), p. 349.

[2] *Ibid.,* pp. 347-378.

[3] *Ibid.*

[4] Mrs. A. M. Townsend, *The Baptist Standard Hymnal* (Nashville: Sunday School Publishing Board, National Baptist Convention, U.S.A., 1924), #700, p. 590.

[5] Whalum, *op. cit.,* p. 349.

[6] James Weldon Johnson and J. Rosamond Johnson, *The Books of American Negro Spirituals,* Book I (New York: A Viking Compass Book, imprint of The Viking Press, 1969), p. 49.

[7] John Hope Franklin, *From Slavery to Freedom,* 3rd ed. (New York: Alfred A. Knopf, Inc., 1967), p. 297.

[8] *Ibid.,* p. 308.

[9] *Ibid.,* pp. 318-320.

[10] Rayford W. Logan, *The Betrayal of the Negro* (New York: Collier Books, imprint of Macmillan, Inc., 1965), pp. 159-160.

[11] William A. Jones, Jr., Spring Lecture, Colgate-Rochester/Bexley Hall/Crozer Theological Seminary, Rochester, New York.

[12] See Logan, *op. cit.,* pp. 23-47.

[13] Franklin, *op. cit.,* p. 327.

[14] John Lovell, Jr., *Black Song: The Forge and the Flame* (New York: Macmillan, Inc., 1972), p. 9.

[15] Edward L. Wheeler, "Beyond One Man: A General Survey of Black Baptist Church History," *Review and Expositor*, vol. 70, no. 3 (Summer, 1973), p. 311.

[16] *Ibid.*, p. 314.

[17] *Ibid.*

[18] *Ibid.*, p. 315.

[19] Townsend, *op. cit.*, p. 4.

[20] *Ibid.*, p. 6.

[21] Townsend, *op. cit.*, #687, p. 587.

[22] *Ibid.*, #685, p. 586.

[23] Ibid., #104, p. 83.

[24] *Ibid.*, #696, p. 589.

Chapter 6

[1] John Hope Franklin, *From Slavery to Freedom*, 3rd ed. (New York: Alfred A. Knopf, Inc., 1967), p. xii.

[2] *Ibid.*, p. 382.

[3] *Ibid.*, p. 383.

[4] *Ibid.*

[5] *Ibid.*, pp. 390-392.

[6] Lerone Bennett, Jr., *Before the Mayflower: A History of the Negro in America, 1619–1964*, rev. ed. (Baltimore: Penguin Books, 1966), p. 240.

[7] Franklin, *op. cit.*, pp. 413-418, 425-432.

[8] *Ibid.*, p. 404.

[9] *Ibid.*, pp. 440-444.

[10] *Ibid.*, p. 445.

[11] *Ibid.*, p. 447.

[12] *Ibid.*, p. 449.

[13] *Ibid.*, pp. 453-454.

[14] *Ibid.*, p. 455.

[15] *Ibid.*, p. 472.

[16] *Ibid.*, p. 479.

[17] *Ibid.*, p. 480.

[18] "If We Must Die," from *Selected Poems of Claude McKay* (Boston: Twayne Publishers, A Division of G. K. Hall & Co., 1953). Reprinted by permission.

[19] Franklin, *op. cit.*, p. 492.

[20] Bennett, *op. cit.*, p. 287.

[21] Aretha Franklin, *Amazing Grace* (New York: Atlantic Records, 1971), CS-2906.

[22] *The Baptist Standard Hymnal, Broadman Hymnal, Tabernacle Hymns, The Service Hymnal, The Cokesbury Worship Hymnal, The American Service Hymnal.*

[23] Mrs. A. M. Townsend, *The Baptist Standard Hymnal* (Nashville:

Sunday School Publishing Board, National Baptist Convention, U.S.A., 1924), #142, p. 111.

[24] Henry H. Mitchell, "Black Improvisation! Real & Imitation," *Freeing the Spirit,* vol. 2, no. 4 (Winter, 1973), p. 39.

Chapter 7

[1] Subtitle of Tony Heilbut's *The Gospel Sound* (New York: Simon and Schuster, Inc., 1971).

[2] Horace C. Boyer, "An Analysis of His Contributions: Thomas A. Dorsey, 'Father of Gospel Music,'" *Black World,* vol. 23, no. 9 (July, 1974), pp. 21-22.

[3] *Ibid.,* p. 22.

[4] Alfred Duckett, "An Interview with Thomas A. Dorsey," *Black World,* vol. 23, no. 9 (July, 1974), p. 13.

[5] Boyer, *op. cit.,* p. 23.

[6] *Ibid.,* p. 21.

[7] Duckett, *op. cit.,* p. 12.

[8] Boyer, *op. cit.,* p. 23.

[9] John Hope Franklin, *From Slavery to Freedom,* 3rd ed. (New York: Alfred A. Knopf, Inc., 1967), pp. 498-499.

[10] Lerone Bennett, Jr., *Before the Mayflower: A History of the Negro in America, 1619–1964,* rev. ed. (Baltimore: Penguin Books, 1966), p. 296.

[11] *Ibid.,* p. 299.

[12] Franklin, *op. cit.,* p. 561.

[13] *Ibid.,* p. 501.

[14] *Ibid.,* p. 525.

[15] Bennett, *op. cit.,* p. 302.

[16] Franklin, *op. cit.,* p. 574.

[17] Bennett, *op. cit.,* p. 306.

[18] *Ibid.,* p. 303.

[19] *Ibid.,* p. 307.

[20] *Ibid.,* p. 556.

[21] Franklin, *op. cit.,* p. 610.

[22] Bennett, *op. cit.,* p. 312.

[23] *Ibid.*

[24] *Ibid.,* p. 313.

[25] Carl Rowan, "The Consequences of Decision," in *Martin Luther King, Jr.: A Profile,* edited by C. Eric Lincoln (New York: Hill & Wang, 1970), pp. 212ff.

[26] Franklin, *op. cit.,* p. 566.

[27] *Ibid.*

[28] W. E. Burghardt Du Bois, *The Souls of Black Folk* (New York: Washington Square Press, 1970), pp. 40, 41.

[29] Pearl Williams-Jones, quoted in Wendel Phillips Whalum, "Black Hymnody," *Review and Expositor*, vol. 70, no. 3 (Summer, 1973), p. 353.

[30] Whalum, *op. cit.*, pp. 345-346.

[31] *Ibid.*, pp. 353-354.

[32] Tony Heilbut, *op. cit.*, p. 11. Copyright © 1971 by Anthony Heilbut. Reprinted by permission of Simon & Schuster, a Division of Gulf & Western Corporation.

[33] *Ibid.*, pp. 12-13.

[34] Whalum, *op. cit.*, p. 354.

[35] Mrs. A. M. Townsend, *The Baptist Standard Hymnal* (Nashville: Sunday School Publishing Board, National Baptist Convention, U.S.A., 1924), #301.

[36] *Big Five Sweet Wonder: Special Song Book, Ecumenical Song Worldwide* (Texarkana, Ark.: Christian Workers Association of America, 1960–1970 ed.), e, #87, p. 26.

[37] Boyer, *op. cit.*, pp. 25, 26.

[38] Thomas A. Dorsey.

[39] W. H. Brewster, Sr.

[40] Roberta Martin.

[41] Heilbut, *op. cit.*, p. 28.

[42] *Ibid.*, pp. 23-24.

[43] *Ibid.*, p. 31.

[44] Doris Akers, Hill & Range.

[45] Roberta Martin.

[46] Yolanda Reed and Robert Anderson.

[47] James Cleveland.

[48] Jessy Dixon.

[49] Sam Cook.

[50] Clinton Utterbach.

Chapter 8

[1] Mrs. A. M. Townsend, *The Baptist Standard Hymnal* (Nashville: Sunday School Publishing Board, National Baptist Convention, U.S.A., 1924), #500, p. 427.

[2] George A. Buttrick, gen. ed., *The Interpreter's Bible* (Nashville: Abingdon Press, 1952), vol. 8, p. 408.

[3] Alfred A. Duckett, "An Interview with Thomas A. Dorsey," *Black World*, vol. 23, no. 9 (July, 1974), pp. 5-6.

[4] Wyatt T. Walker, "The Soulful Journey of the Negro Spiritual: Freedom's Song," *Negro Digest*, July, 1963, pp. 93-94.

[5] Doris Akers.

[6] Townsend, *op. cit.*, #700, p. 590.

[7] Refrain of Doris Akers's tune.

[8] Traditional stanza paraphrased from spiritual; used interchangeably with different songs.

[9] Sterling Plumpp, *Black Rituals* (Chicago: Third World Press, 1972), p. 88.

[10] Tony Heilbut, *The Gospel Sound* (New York: Simon and Schuster, Inc., 1971), p. 28.

[11] *Southland Spirituals* (Chicago: The Rodeheaver Hall-Mack Co., 1936), p. 17.

[12] Eugene Genovese, *Roll, Jordan, Roll* (New York: Pantheon Books, div. of Random House, 1974), p. 280.

[13] *Ibid.,* title page.

[14] Ortiz Walton, *Music: Black, White and Blue* (New York: William A. Morrow & Company, Inc., 1972), p. 27.

[15] Philip Sterling and Rayford Logan, *Four Took Freedom* (Garden City, N.Y.: Zenith Books, imprint of Doubleday & Company, Inc., 1967), pp. 9, 10, 30.

[16] Walker, *op. cit.,* pp. 84-85.

[17] *Ibid.,* p. 86.

[18] The author served as executive director of the Southern Christian Leadership Conference, 1960–1964.

[19] Walker, *op. cit.,* p. 92.

[20] Lerone Bennett, Jr., *Before the Mayflower: A History of the Negro in America, 1619-1964,* rev. ed. (Baltimore: Penguin Books, 1966), p. 345.

[21] Administrative staff, SCLC: in order, program director; director, Citizenship Education Program; direct action specialist; national secretary of SCLC; administrative assistant to Wyatt Tee Walker; and treasurer, SCLC.

[22] The Albany Movement, Dr. W. G. Anderson, president; Nashville (Tenn.) Christian Leadership Council, Rev. Kelly Miller Smith, president; Petersburg (Va.) Improvement Association, Rev. Wyatt Tee Walker, president; and the Montgomery Improvement Association, Dr. Martin Luther King, Jr., president.

[23] From *The Service Hymnal* (Chicago: Hope Publishing Company, 1935), p. 373.

[24] Townsend, *op. cit.,* #488, p. 415.

Index